THE PENAL REMEDIES OF THE CODE OF CANON LAW

This dissertation was approved by the Reverend John Rogg Schmidt, A. B., J. C. D., LL. B., Professor of Canon Law, as director and by the Reverend Romaeus W. O'Brien, O. Carm., J. C. D. and the Reverend John J. McGrath, A. B., LL. B., J. C. D. as readers.

THE CATHOLIC UNIVERSITY OF AMERICA
CANON LAW STUDIES
No. 404

THE PENAL REMEDIES OF THE CODE OF CANON LAW

A DISSERTATION

Submitted to the Faculty of the School of Canon Law of The Catholic University of America in Partial Fulfilment of the Requirements for the Degree of Doctor of Canon Law

BY

REVEREND PAUL L. LOVE, A. B., J. C. L.
A Priest of the Archdiocese of Baltimore

THE CATHOLIC UNIVERSITY OF AMERICA PRESS
WASHINGTON, D. C.
1960

Nihil Obstat:

JOANNES R. SCHMIDT, A. B., J. C. D., LL. B.
Censor Deputatus

Imprimatur:

✠ FRANCISCUS P. KEOUGH, D. D.
Archiepiscopus Baltimorensis

die 6 aprilis 1960

PRINTED IN THE UNITED STATES OF AMERICA
BY J. H. FURST COMPANY, BALTIMORE, MARYLAND

DEDICATED

TO

THE SACRED HEART OF JESUS

Model of Justice and Mercy

FOREWORD

The trend in many modern systems of civil penal law toward the effective prevention of crime as well as its repression also has an established place in the coactive legislation of the Church. Among the best of the Church's measures in this regard are the penal remedies of the Code of Canon Law. These remedies are both crime-preventive and crime-repressive. While not overlooking their usefulness as equitable punishments for crimes which have already been committed, the Church especially prescribes the penal remedies with a view that these measures, when applied in opportune time, will effect the adjustment of conduct which is needed to forestall the commission or repetition of delicts and their accompanying grave consequences.

The penal remedies of the Code of Canon Law—warning, rebuke, precept, and surveillance—are the subject of this dissertation. The specific objectives of this work are twofold: 1) to present the general concept and characteristics of these remedies in so far as they constitute a legal unit or institute in the present legislation of the Church; and 2) to study their application as found in canons 2306-2311. With the thought that a detailed consideration of the various phases of use for any specific remedy as indicated throughout the Code would supply ample material for possible future dissertations in this series of Canon Law Studies, this aspect was intentionally eliminated from the scope of the present work.

The writer is grateful to His Excellency, the Most Reverend Francis P. Keough, D. D., Archbishop of Baltimore, for his paternal interest and kindness which made possible the opportunity for advanced study in Canon Law at the Catholic University of America. Gratitude is expressed also to the Faculty of the School of Canon Law for their scholarly guidance and gracious assistance. Special acknowledgment is due the Reverend John Rogg Schmidt, A. B., J. C. D., LL. B., for his counsel and direction of this dissertation. To the several Priests, Sisters and members of the laity whose friendship, prayers, and assistance meant so much during these years of study, a most cordial word of appreciation is extended. Lastly, the writer welcomes this opportunity to publicly acknowledge the constant devotion and prayerful interest of his father, mother, and brother, who have been an abiding source of encouragement not only for this project, but for every assignment and undertaking.

TABLE OF CONTENTS

CHAPTER III

CHAPTER IV

CHAPTER I

THE JURIDIC FOUNDATION FOR THE PENAL REMEDIES OF THE CODE

The juridic foundation for the penal remedies of the Code of Canon Law is evident at least implicitly[1] in the legislation of the Council of Trent[2] (1545-1563), and explicitly in the Instructions of the Holy See, *Sacra Haec*[3] and *Cum Magnopere*.[4] The use of such canonical remedies was also prescribed by the decrees of the Third Plenary Council of Baltimore[5] (1884).

ARTICLE I. THE LEGISLATION OF THE COUNCIL OF TRENT

The Fathers of the Council of Trent (1545-1563), assembled in the thirteenth session, gave a clear though merely implicit recommendation for the use of penal remedies.[6] After noting that it is the duty of Bishops to correct their subjects, it is further recalled that this should be accomplished in the role and spirit of a true

1 Cf. Cocchi, *Commentarium in Codicem Iuris Canonici* (4. ed., Taurinorum Augustae: Marietti, 1938) VIII, 207, n. 121 [hereafter cited *Commentarium*]; De Meester, *Iuris Canonici et Iuris Canonico-Civilis Compendium* (Tom. III, Pars II, Brussels: Desclée, 1928) 227 [hereafter cited *Compendium*]; Regatillo, *Institutiones Iuris Canonici* (4. ed., Sal Terrae: Santander, 1951) II, 532, n. 957 [hereafter cited *Institutiones*].

2 *Canones et Decreta Concilii Tridentini* (Taurini, 1913).

3 S. C. Ep. et Reg., instr. 11 iun. 1880 [hereafter cited *Sacra Haec*]—*Codicis Iuris Canonici Fontes*, cura et studio Emi Petri Card. Gasparri editi (9 vols., Romae [postea Civitate Vaticano]: Typis Polyglottis Vaticanis, 1923-1939; Vols. VII-IX, ed. cura et studio Emi Iustiniani Card. Serédi), n. 2005 [hereafter cited *Fontes*].

4 S. C. de Prop. Fide, instr., a. 1883—*Fontes*, n. 4900; *Collectanea S. Congregationis de Propaganda Fide* (2 vols., Romae: Typographia S. C. de Propaganda Fide, 1907), n. 1586 [hereafter cited *Collectanea*].

5 *Acta et Decreta Concilii Plenarii Baltimorensis Tertii A.D. MDCCCLXXXIV* (Baltimorae: Typis Joannis Murphy et Sociorum, 1886), p. 176-178, nn. 308-310.

6 Conc. Trident., sess. XIII, *de ref.*, c. 1.

shepherd of souls. Bishops are urged to love their subjects as children and brothers and to *strive by exhortation and admonition to deter them from what is unlawful.* For those of the faithful who sin, the Bishop is to follow the pattern of St. Paul and ". . . reprove, entreat, rebuke them in all kindness and patience,"[7] since kindness often effects more than severity, exhortation more than threat, charity more than force.[8] If the gravity of the offense requires a punishment, then rigor should be tempered with gentleness, judgment with mercy, severity with clemency.

While the use of measures of discipline by the Church is seen to be both necessary and salutary for the faithful (as a means of correcting the offender and deterring all from the commission of offenses), it should be administered without harshness. To provide such discipline, the Council again implicitly refers to the use of the penal remedies by its observation that mild means are to be first employed in the correction of the faithful, and only after these fail are the more severe measures to be used progressively. The Council of Trent states:

> . . . it is the duty of a shepherd, being both diligent and kind, to first apply *mild anodynes* to the disorder of the sheep, and afterwards, if the gravity of the disorder should demand it, to proceed to use sharper and *more severe remedies.* In the event that even these prove ineffective in removing the disorders, then the shepherd is to free the other sheep from the danger of contagion.[9]

Thus, in effect, the Council advocates the use of mild remedies as a means of protecting the social order of the Church. If these prove ineffective, then the more severe remedies are to follow before the heavy penalties of the Church (e. g. interdict, excommunication, etc.) are to be employed.

Besides these principal references from Trent, the Council also provides ample legislation which continues and reenforces what may be considered as the beginnings of the penal remedies contained in the use of the *monitio* employed in the legislation of previous

[7] II Timothy, 4, 2.

[8] C. 6, D. XLV.

[9] Conc. Trident., sess. XIII, *de ref.*, c. 1; cf. also cc. 16, 17, C. XXIV, q. 3. Italics added by present writer.

centuries. This legislation frequently prescribed the *monitio* to be used in cases where a delict or grave abuse had already been committed. It seems that to some degree such use of the *monitio* shared in the characteristics of the repressive penal remedies of the Code.[10] Among those instances which may be cited from the Council, appropriate admonitions are prescribed for cases of non-residence of clerics,[11] clerics abandoning the ecclesiastical dress,[12] neglect of hospitality by those obliged to give it by reason of their benefice,[13] concubinage by the laity[14] and by clerics,[15] religious superiors of regulars neglecting to see that their subjects follow their Rule,[16] and clerics leading a scandalous life.[17] Likewise the Twenty-second session of the Council of Trent, in speaking of the improvement of the life and conduct of clerics, states: ". . . the holy council ordains that those things which have in the past been frequently and wholesomely enacted by the supreme pontiffs and holy councils concerning the adherence to the life, conduct, dress and learning of clerics, as also the avoidance of luxury, feastings, dances, gambling, sports and all sorts of crime and secular pursuits, shall in the future be observed under the same or greater penalties to be imposed at the discretion of the Ordinary."[18] The correction of abuses in many of these matters normally required the use of admonitions before more severe penalties could be inflicted.[19]

10 It is the opinion of the present writer, however, that, in accord with the penal principle *admonitio praecedere debet vindictam*, such use of the *monitio* was prescribed chiefly to safeguard the administration of justice and to establish contumacy rather than to be a measure of crime-prevention, the objective of the penal remedies of the Code. Nonetheless, this latter characteristic cannot be definitely considered as excluded from being at least a partial objective of such legislation.

11 Conc. Trident., sess. VI, *de ref.*, c. 1.

12 Conc. Trident., sess. XIV, *de ref.*, c. 6.

13 Conc. Trident., sess. XXV, *de ref.*, c. 8.

14 Conc. Trident., sess. XXIV, *de ref.*, c. 8.

15 Conc. Trident., sess. XXV, *de ref.*, c. 14.

16 Conc. Trident., sess. XXI, *de ref.*, c. 8.

17 Conc. Trident., sess. XXI, *de ref.*, c. 6.

18 Conc. Trident., sess. XX, *de ref.*, c. 1.

19 Many of these abuses in the clerical state are considered in Book III, Title 1, *de vita et honestate clericorum*, in the *Decretales* of Gregory IX, *in*

Therefore it may be said that while they were not as explicit as subsequent legislation, the decrees of the Council of Trent did implicitly recommend the use of the penal remedies,[20] and explicitly commanded the use of admonitions which may have shared partially, at least, in the characteristics of the repressive penal remedies of the Code.

The pertinent legislation subsequent to the Council of Trent is embodied in the two Instructions of the Holy See, *Sacra Haec* and

VI°, and *in Clem.* Some of these evils (e. g. the conducting of profane spectacles in churches) did not require an admonition before a more severe punishment was inflicted (cf. c. 12, X, *de vita et honestate clericorum,* III, 1). Admonitions were required, however, for cases of clerics who were involved in: gambling and games of chance (*glossa ordinaria s. v. aleas*; c. 15, X, *de vita et honestate clericorum,* III, 1); carrying weapons in warfare (*glossa ordinaria ad* c. 2, X, *de vita et honestate clericorum,* III, 1); intemperance and drinking-bouts (c. 14, X, *de vita et honestate clericorum,* III, 1); acting as jesters and buffoons (c. *un, de vita et honestate clericorum,* III, 1, in VI°); secular business, secular offices, tavern keeping, butcher business, etc. (c. 1, *de vita et honestate clericorum,* III, 1, *in Clem.*; c. 16, X, *de vita et honestate clericorum*); frequenting the monasteries of nuns (c. 8, X, *de vita et honestate clericorum,* III, 1).

Besides the legislation contained in Book III, Title I, other examples of the use of admonitions for clerics before more severe measures were taken against them may be cited for cases of: non-residence and neglect of benefices (c. 28, X, *de appelationibus recusationibus et relationibus,* II, 28); concubinage (cc. 4, 6, 8, X, *de cohabitatione clericorum et mulierum,* III, 2); harassing others with repeated physical violence (c. 1, X, *de clerico percussore,* V, 25); abandoning the use of the tonsure and the clerical garb (c. 45, X, *de sententia excommunicationis,* V, 39); continuing to perform the functions of a cleric after being suspended (c. 3, X, *de clerico excommunicato, deposito vel interdicto ministrante,* V, 27); vagrant monks refusing to return to their monastery (c. 17, C. XVI, q. 1).

It is said that these cases *normally* required an admonition, because there also were crimes whose circumstances required the immediate use of a severe penalty, e. g. cases involving *ipso facto* suspension or excommunication; cases involving a *delictum momentaneum* which result in *infamia facti*; cases which produced *notorium facti* and thus required an immediate penalty [cf. F. Suarez, *Disputationum De Censuris in Communi* (Tom. V, Disp. III, Sect. VIII, Lugduni: sumptibus Horatii Cardon, 1608), p. 34 ff.; P. L. Love, *The Nature and Use of the Monitio in the Corpus Iuris Canonici* (*An Historical Study of the Beginnings of the Penal Remedies*), The Catholic University of America Canon Law Studies (Washington, D. C., typewritten licentiate dissertation, 1958), p. 40-43.]

20 Cf. Cocchi, *Commentarium,* VIII, 207, n. 121.

Cum Magnopere. Portions of these enactments are seen to be the immediate precursors of the legislation concerning the penal remedies of the Code of Canon Law. Since their provisions are the direct subject matter for interpreting the provisions of the Code,[21] these Instructions are the burden of the two articles immediately following.

Article II. The Instruction *Sacra Haec*

The Instruction *Sacra Haec*[22] may well be called the *Magna Charta* of the penal remedies. Issued by the Sacred Congregation for Bishops and Regulars in 1880, it presented a new summary procedure for handling the disciplinary and criminal cases of clerics.[23] Besides this summary process, it also expressly prescribed the use of preventive as well as repressive remedies as canonical disciplinary measures. It is this latter feature which attracts our special attention and merits our close consideration. While there have been some modifications of its contents by the subsequent legislation of the Code of Canon Law, certain provisions of this Instruction still form the nucleus for any thorough understanding of the penal remedies of the Code.

21 Cf. cc. 6, 2°-4°; 23.

22 S. C. Ep. et Reg., instr. 11 iun. 1880—Fontes, n. 2005.

23 In his editor's preface to *Canonical Procedure* published in 1887, Messmer claims that this Instruction was sent to the Bishops of Italy. On page 23 of the Introduction in the same book, he also alludes to the fact that it was sent only to the Bishops of Italy by declaring that at that time the provisions of the Instruction were formal law only for Italy.

Smith takes a different view in *New Procedure,* published in the same year (1887). He claims that the Instruction *Sacra Haec* contains dispensations from the old procedure granted by the Holy See to Bishops of European countries (cf. p. 14). He does not specify which countries, or whether all countries of Europe are included.

Regatillo declares that this Instruction was issued for Italy, but in practice it was declared for the whole Church (*Institutiones,* II, 532). This view would have to be understood, of course, to refer to only those parts of the Church which were subject to the Sacred Congregation for Bishops and Regulars at that time.

The text of the Instruction itself gives no evidence to whom it was addressed. While it is clear that it had application to the clergy of Italy, it cannot be said with certainty what other countries, if any, were formally intended to be included.

Although the Instruction *Sacra Haec* became formal law for Italy and possibly other European countries, its acceptance and efficacy soon gave ample evidence that the results and the reform produced by the Instruction would not remain confined to Europe. Within the brief span of three years *Sacra Haec* was substantially accepted by the Sacred Congregation for the Propagation of the Faith and issued as a directive for the handling of criminal and disciplinary causes of clerics in the United States under the title of *Instructio Cum Magnopere.*[24] The provisions of this latter document became particular law for the United States, and some of its specifications were also included in the *Acta* of the Third Plenary Council of Baltimore in the year following its issuance (1884).[25]

According to Messmer, "The Instruction of 1880 appears like a new creation. It is not a mere furbishing up of old material or putting together of what had once been parts of various canonical processes. It is a new legislation in spirit, character and form. Although the matter is gathered from older forms of trials, yet there is evidently a new substantial form to unite them into a new canonical procedure that has no like in all the former laws."[26] While someone's reaction to these statements may at first be one of doubt accompanied with an inclination to believe that the author was "carried away" by his subject and overreached himself by exaggerating its character, yet a careful study of *Sacra Haec* leads the reader to a full agreement with Messmer's opinion.

The Instruction *Sacra Haec* contains an Introduction and forty-four articles. Eight of these articles treat of the canonical remedies (art. 2-9 incl.), and the subsequent articles are concerned with the summary judicial process (art. 10-44 incl.). The Introduction and article 1 apply equally to both categories.

In the Introduction the Sacred Congregation for Bishops and Regulars gives its two-fold reasons for issuing the norms of *Sacra Haec*: (1) Mature consideration has produced the observation that conditions in the world are such that the Church is almost everywhere impeded from applying its external action to ecclesiastical matters and persons. (2) It is realized also that there are many

[24] S. C. de Prop. Fide, instr. a. 1883—*Fontes*, n. 4900.

[25] Cf. Conc. Pl. Balt. III., nn. 308-310—*Acta et Decreta*, p. 176-178.

[26] *Canonical Procedure*, p. 9.

dioceses which lack the appropriate means and facilities to establish a regular ecclesiastical curia to employ the full canonical process.[27] Mindful of these conditions, the Sacred Congregation is all the while concerned that the substance of justice may remain safe and sound, and that the canonical regularity and uniformity of procedure will be preserved.[28] The Instruction is issued, therefore, with the clear intention of keeping at least the canonical discipline of the clergy within the influence of ecclesiastical control, and the Bishops are reminded of their duty in this regard.[29]

What actually is the Congregation stating here? It seems to say that since the times have changed, the Church's method in its exercise of some phases of its coercive power is changing also. In an attempt to reaffirm and strengthen its prerogative of correcting ecclesiastical matters and persons in the external forum,[30] the Church is partly dispensing from the old procedure and replacing it with the provisions of *Sacra Haec.* These provisions of *Sacra Haec* are thus looked upon as substitutes or replacements to be used at times instead of the more complicated formal procedure. Both the old and the new measures are considered to be juridic methods of discipline. As replacement for the older method, it is logical to conclude that the provisions of the Instruction would have the same binding force as those which it replaces. It is hardly thinkable that the Church would substitute a weaker and therefore less effective method of discipline as a means of reaffirming and strengthening its prerogative to exercise coercive power over ecclesiastical matters and persons. The new measures, as well as the old, are juridic methods of discipline in the external forum.

The first article of *Sacra Haec* presents a straight-forward statement of the superior-to-subject relationship which exists between the Ordinary and his clergy. By inference, at least, it also contains the reciprocal obligation of clerical obedience to the Ordinary. Special emphasis is placed upon the role of shepherd on the part of the Ordinary. As a true shepherd he must look to the preservation

27 Cf. *Sacra Haec,* Introduction.

28 *Ibid.*

29 *Sacra Haec,* n. 1.

30 *Sacra Haec,* Introduction: . . . externam explicit suum actionem super materias et personas ecclesiasticas. . . .

of order in his flock; and this duty, in turn, requires a vigilance over his clergy, the special members of the fold entrusted to his care. In fulfilling this responsibility the Ordinary must watch over the clergy's manner of living and, when need arises, he should resort to *canonical remedies* both to: (1) prevent and (2) eliminate any disturbance of order among them.[31]

The canonical remedies which the Ordinary is to employ in order to prevent and eliminate any disturbance of order among his clergy are further specified in article n. 2. Here it is stated that there are two types of these remedies: (1) PREVENTIVE and (2) REPRESSIVE. While each type has its own approach to a particular problem, there is no indication given that one is more characteristic of the concept of a canonical remedy than the other. Both are canonical remedies. Both are intended to be used ". . . to prevent and eliminate disturbances of order among them [the clergy]."[32]

The PREVENTIVE remedies are intended to impede and forestall an approaching evil, and to remove the stimuli of scandal, the voluntary occasions and the proximate causes of committing delicts.[33]

31 Cf. *Sacra Haec*, n. 1. Since the term *Ordinary* is used here, it is evident that the power to use these remedies is restricted to a cleric having the power of jurisdiction in the external forum. It may be further noted that the Introduction of *Sacra Haec* states specifically that the faculties contained in the provisions of the Instruction are granted to the *local Ordinaries*.

It seems reasonable to conclude that the term *Ordinary* used in art. n. 1 does not include the Vicar General. In the latter years of the nineteenth century the extent of jurisdiction possessed by the Vicar General was not as clear as it is today (Cf. Messmer, *Canonical Procedure*, p. 35-36 for a nineteenth century view of the jurisdiction of the Vicar General). There is good indication from the text of the Instruction that in such matters the role of the Vicar General is limited to that of being an official witness when a precept is issued by the chancellor (art. n. 8), and to act as the guardian of secrecy if the case demands it (art. n. 8, § 2). Smith observes that the local Ordinary could, of course, depute the Vicar General by a special commission to employ these disciplinary measures according to the norms of law—*Elements of Ecclesiastical Law* (3. ed., 3 vols., New York: Benziger Brothers, 1888), III, 153.

32 *Sacra Haec*, n. 1.

33 Cf. *Sacra Haec*, n. 2.

The REPRESSIVE remedies strive to bring a return to moral good health and well-being in cases where a delict has already been committed. They seek to recall the delinquent to the point that he will regain his wisdom and balance of values and will repair the evil effects of his crimes.[34]

It is the opinion of the present writer that in article n. 2 a new aspect is presented in the penal legislation of the Church. Prior to the appearance of this Instruction it seems that any canonical remedy was thought of in terms of a repressive entity and was employed only after a crime had been committed. If there were any preventive aspect at all, it lay in the fact that the remedy tried to prevent the continuation of a crime. Any efforts to prevent the commission of the first crime were not canonical in their status, but resulted from charitable counsels. Now, however, *Sacra Haec* makes it clear that remedies which are canonical may be employed to forestall the first crime as well as to impede its continuation.[35] The preventive remedies are given full status as canonical remedies. They thus become mild, but nonetheless juridic methods of discipline in the external forum. As has been noted previously, this status seems verified by the very intention of issuing the Instruction as outlined in its Introduction.

There seems to be a natural progression or hierarchy of procedure with regard to the use of the remedies of *Sacra Haec*. If the respective conditions for their use are present, first the preventive remedies are to be applied and then, if needed, the repressive remedies are to follow. One remedy is, then, the complement of the other. This methodical procedure follows the Congregation's intention to achieve simplicity and effectiveness in its manner of discipline.

Not only do the preventive remedies demand obedience of the person receiving them; but in the event of disobedience, they may be subsequently enforced by at least summary judicial action and subsequent punishment. No longer is there a question here of merely a charitable urging, or chiding, to be careful of that habit or this occasion, or else it could lead to some more serious consequences. By *Sacra Haec* the preventive remedies and their canoni-

34 *Ibid.*

35 Cf. *Sacra Haec*, n. 2.

cal application have been lifted from the sphere of merely fraternal or paternal relationship and have been given a truly canonical standing as a partial replacement for the older formal procedure. What does this result imply? It means that obedience is due, as a matter of legal justice, when the preventive remedies are issued to someone. These mild methods of discipline thus have greater force, greater obligation, and greater efficacy, it is hoped, than they could ever possibly have without their canonical status. Now they produce obligations to obey imposed by an Ordinary who as a matter of justice is exercising his power in the external forum as a public official of the Church in order to preserve order in that society.

Article 3 of the Instruction reminds the Ordinary of his conscientious obligation and yet also gives him much discretionary power in the use of these canonical remedies. Apparently the matter is left to the dictates of his conscience and to his prudent judgment.[36] In the event that he decides to use them, however, his actions may not be completely arbitrary. On the contrary, he must apply them ". . . according to the prescripts of the canons and [according to] the gravity and circumstances of the case."[37]

The subsequent article (n. 4) lists the principle preservative remedies which are available to the Ordinary: spiritual exercises, warnings and precepts. Apparently this list is not intended to be an exhaustive or exclusive enumeration. The authors[38] are quick to point out that the use of *praecipue* connotes the possibility that other remedies may be used as well. Lega approaches this subject from the point of view that the Instruction certainly does not intend to limit the power of the Ordinaries, but rather to point the way to the correct application of the penal measures.[39] The proper use of the correct remedy at the right time is the main

[36] *Sacra Haec*, n. 3: Conscientiae et prudentiae Ordinarii horum remediorum incumbit applicatio. . . .

[37] *Sacra Haec*, n. 3: . . . iuxta canonum praescriptiones et casuum adiunctorumque gravitatem.

[38] E. g. Lega, *Praelectiones de Iudiciis Ecclesiasticis* (4 vols., Romae: Typis Vaticanis, 1901), IV, 351, n. 281 [hereafter cited *Praelectiones*]; Wernz, *Ius Decretalium* (3. ed., 6 vols., Prati, 1913), VI, 259 [hereafter cited *Ius Decretalium*].

[39] *Praelectiones*, IV, 351, n. 281.

thing. Thus he does not believe that there is any intention to confine the Ordinary by an obligation of using these three, and only these three species of remedies.

The withholding of conferral of an office by a Bishop in order to correct a cleric's manner of acting seems to Lega to be a very effective measure. While not being either a canonical warning or precept, he believes that such a withholding of appointment to an office would be a useful preservative remedy.[40] In the same manner, he observes that the denial of letters of permission to leave the diocese, which are readily granted to other clerics, may be a good means to correct the arrogance or enmity of a particular cleric. Lega sees this method and other similar ones to be effective preservative remedies depending on the specific circumstances of particular abuses. Therefore he concludes that there are many other measures which may be employed as preservative remedies besides the ones listed in the Instruction.[41]

In effect then, the Ordinary is instructed that when he decides that the conditions for applying a preservative remedy are present, he should especially consider one of these particular measures: spiritual exercises, warning or precept. The list of remedies in *Sacra Haec* seems, therefore, to be merely demonstrative and not exclusive.

It may be pointed out also that the Instruction lists these remedies as being preservative measures.[42] This term is generic and seems to include both the preventive and repressive aspects of the canonical remedies as presented in the preceding articles 1 and 2.[43] By way of anticipation, it may be stated that the use of the generic concept of preservative measures very closely parallels the concept and uses of the penal remedies in the Code, which strive to preserve

[40] *Ibid.*

[41] *Ibid.*

[42] *Sacra Haec,* n. 4: Mediis, quae praeservant, ...

[43] *Sacra Haec,* n. 1: Ordinario pastorale onus incumbit disciplinam correctionemque clericorum a se dependentium curandi super eorumdem vitae rationem vigilando, remediisque utendo canonicis ad praecavendas apud eosdem et eliminandas ordinis perturbationes.

N. 2: Ex his remediis alia praeveniunt, alia reprimunt et medelam afferunt. . . .

order in the society by preventing both progression into crime and greater punishment.[44]

The next five articles (n. 5-9) of *Sacra Haec* present what may be termed the *modus procedendi* for the application of the canonical remedies contained in this Instruction. This material may be outlined as follows:

1. Preliminary summary investigation
2. Species of Canonical Warnings
   a. *In forma paterna et secreta*
   b. *In forma legali*
   c. Scholion: Warnings with the threat of penalty.
3. Precept
4. Penal measures.

1. PRELIMINARY SUMMARY INVESTIGATION

Once the Ordinary has become aware of a situation which may need correction, he must give it his attention. Before any definite action may be taken, however, a summary investigation of the facts must be made in order to determine the truth of the matters involved. This proceeding must be done simply and without any formality,[45] but cautiously, in order to guard against any rash defamation of the suspected person's good name. Whenever it is possible and not too inconvenient, the Ordinary should conduct the inquiry personally, so as not to give the matter the slightest publicity. If however the cause of truth and justice is better served by having the inquiry made by a less conspicuous person, the Ordinary may act through a prudent and trustworthy delegate. The very nature of this investigation requires that secrecy must be conscientiously observed. This precaution is especially required of all persons concerned, when in more difficult cases witnesses must be informally examined and possibly the assistance of experts employed. Above all things the Ordinary should proceed with great caution and carefulness ". . . lest he unnecessarily injure an

[44] Cf. Cc. 1933, § 4; 1947-1953; 2223, § 3, 3°; 2224, § 2; 2234; 2306-2311.

[45] *Canonical Procedure*, p. 146.

ecclesiastic and from outward appearances consider and treat him as guilty before his offense has been proved." [46]

If the investigation yields no evidence for the truth of the suspected abuse, or if the results are such that only a slight suspicion is produced, Messmer believes that then the acts of the investigation which may have been made ought to be destroyed.[47]

On the other hand, if any substantial evidence has been found, the Ordinary must make a notation of it and proceed with the matter as he judges is dictated by necessity. This notation is intended to crystalize his motives for taking action. It furthermore serves as a protection for the Ordinary in the event that he is required by superior authority to give an account or even possibly a defense of his disciplinary action towards the cleric.[48]

While not prescribed by the Instruction, Messmer adds in his footnote to this matter, that the results of the summary investigation together with the notations of the Ordinary must be kept in the diocesan archives in accord with the prescriptions appearing in the *Acta Sanctae Sedis*.[49] This being the case, they should be kept in the secret archives since these matters are by their very nature secret.

After the inquiry has been made and has yielded substantial evidence that corrective measures are required, the Ordinary will decide how to proceed: whether by canonical remedies or judicial means; whether by severe or milder measures.[50] To a great extent the subject matter, the circumstances, the reasonable hope for results or the apparent fruitlessness of the effort, and the possible danger which would be involved if there were a delay, will have much bearing on this decision.

If one were to look for a general rule for the application of disciplinary measures, he might well consider the opinion of Messmer. He states that the Bishop should not proceed to a trial

46 *Canonical Procedure*, p. 147.

47 Cf. *Canonical Procedure*, p. 147, note 2. This pre-Code method seems contrary to the present legislation of c. 1946, § 2, 1°-2°.

48 Cf. *Sacra Haec*, n. 5.

49 *Acta Sanctae Sedis*, XV (1882), 380; *Canonical Procedure*, p. 147, note 2.

50 *Sacra Haec*, nn. 3, 9, 10.

as long as there is no necessity or where there is a chance to otherwise remedy the evil. He believes the mind of the Church is reluctant to employ its judicial system unless it is truly necessary: "*Horret enim ecclesia judiciorum arma.*"[51]

2. SPECIES OF CANONICAL WARNINGS.

If the Orinary decides to resort to the use of canonical warnings, there are two types at his disposal: a) *in forma paterna et secreta*; b) *in forma legali*.

A distinction is made here between a canonical paternal warning and a canonical legal warning. It should be noted that both of these remedies are called canonical. On this point Lega observes that although a warning might be fraternal, paternal or charitable, it is called canonical in so far as it is given by the power of public authority.[52]

The difference between these two species of canonical warnings lies in the fact that they are given either in the absence or presence of witnesses. In accord with the pattern outlined in the Gospel,[53] they are given *in forma paterna et secreta* if no witnesses are present ["between thee and him alone"], and *in forma legali* if witnesses are used to verify and solemnize the warning ["take with thee one or two more so that on the word of two or three witnesses each word may be confirmed"].[54]

a. *In Forma Paterna et Secreta*

A paternal and secret warning is given by the Ordinary when he warns a person of his obligation to do something or abstain from something by persuading him that he should keep his conduct good. In this warning the Ordinary might appeal to the person's good name and reputation which otherwise may be gravely endangered, his usefulness, his conscience and peace of soul, his fine record in the past, his duties of state of life and similar motivations

[51] *Canonical Procedure*, p. 148, note 2. He believes this conclusion also to be the mind of the Third Plenary Council of Baltimore, n. 309.

[52] *Praelectiones*, IV, 353, n. 284.

[53] Matthew, 18, 15-17.

[54] Cf. *infra* for development of this distinction; also Messmer, *Canonical Procedure*, p. 151.

of conduct. Whatever the specific approach may be, the Ordinary acts with the solicitude of a true shepherd or as a father speaking confidently to his son, giving him warning without censuring anger and without fear of punishment. The approach is evidenced by nothing less than good will for his subject.[55] As its very name indicates, paternal charity and mildness are characteristic features of this warning. Thus, the Bishop will act as secretly as possible in order to show by the very form and in his manner that he is acting as a father, not a judge.[56]

Most often the warnings deal with some clerical obligations e. g. not conversing with someone, not visiting some particular person or place, observing the obligation of residence, not cohabiting, correctly and piously fulfilling the various duties associated with the divine offices and ecclesiastical benefices, etc.

It would seem that the warning *in forma paterna et secreta* is very useful for cases where a fault or delict has not fully been proven to exist, but where a well-founded suspicion of its existence remains.[57] If the person who is warned is guilty, he is thus expected to cooperate with the remedy and avoid the delict in the future. On the other hand, this warning affords the innocent person an excellent opportunity to prove his innocence and clear himself from all suspicion and taint of guilt. In both cases the secrecy and lack of witnesses protects the good name of the person as much as possible.[58]

The paternal and secret warning as well as the other remedies may not be given unless the Bishop has serious indications about the guilt of the person to be corrected.[59] Full proof is not required to be produced in the investigation of the case. Rather the Bishop may proceed with the warning as long as the serious indications result from at least *semi-plena* proof.[60] It is evident that this *semi-*

55 Cf. Lega, *Praelectiones,* IV, 354, n. 285.

56 Messmer, *Canonical Procedure,* p. 150.

57 Messmer, *Canonical Procedure,* p. 149.

58 Lega, *Praelectiones,* IV, 357, n. 287.

59 Lega, *op. cit.,* 356, n. 287.

60 Cf. *Acta Sanctae Sedis,* XV (1882), p. 378: "Semiplena illa est quae facit quidem aliquam fidem rei gestae, sed non tantam, quae sufficiat ad definiendas controversias, uti est probatio per unum testem, per con-

plena proof cannot of necessity be determined by an absolute standard of measurement, because the gravity of the evidence is relatively greater or less depending upon the circumstances of fact and of the persons involved.[61] The decision whether or not such proof has been ascertained, and that a warning should be given, must therefore be left to the prudent judgment of the Bishop.

Since this warning is given in a secret and paternal manner, it is thought to be more desirable to have the Bishop act personally face-to-face with the person being warned.[62] If, however, the Bishop is unable to do so or does not wish to call the person into his presence and speak to him personally, the Instruction provides that he may give the warning in a letter or by an intermediary.[63]

Lega notes that it may happen that, because of friendship or excessive kindness and similar emotions, the giving of the warning face-to-face may be the occasion for the person who is being corrected to succeed in covering up his fault with weak excuses and thereby to hinder the Bishop from performing his duty.[64] In these and similar cases the other methods of giving a warning are very desirable and useful.

When the secret and paternal warning is sent by letter, it must be done in such a manner that it will not be identified as the more severe warning *in forma legali.* There should, therefore, be no formalities, such as the signature of the chancellor or other ecclesiastical notary, and the use of the official seal. In sending the letter, some evidence of its receipt or refusal must be retained by the Bishop. If the letter is sent by a messenger of the curia or some other suitable person, a memorandum to this effect must be made, together with a notation of its acceptance or refusal. The same may otherwise be accomplished by using registered mail with request for a return receipt, if this method is feasible in the particular locality.[65]

fessionem extrajudicialem, per scripturam privatam, per fugam rei qui debuisset respondere, per famam et hujusmodi."

61 Cf. Lega, *Praelectiones*, IV, 357, n. 287.

62 Messmer, *Canonical Procedure*, p. 150.

63 *Sacra Haec*, n. 6.

64 *Praelectiones*, IV, 355, n. 285.

65 *Sacra Haec*, n. 14.

Sacra Haec also provides that the warning may be given by an intermediary acting as delegate of the Bishop.[66] Due to its paternal and secret nature, the choice of a delegate would, of course, be limited to someone who is well qualified for the assignment by reason of his tact, prudence and trustworthiness. He should be of such a character and standing in the community that he is respected and accepted to be someone who is worthy to speak in the name of the Bishop.[67]

It is the opinion of Messmer[68] that while article 6 of *Sacra Haec* allows the Bishop to employ an intermediary, he should avail himself of this right only when reasons make such an action appear necessary and useful. While this view seems to be very sensible, there actually appears to be nothing in the text of the Instruction which would indicate that a necessity would be required before the Bishop could employ the services of a delegate. It is reasonable to presume, of course, that he ordinarily would not resort to such means unless he saw that by reason of the nature of the case or the person involved, it would be advisable to do so.

It is the obvious intention of the Instruction that this warning should remain secret. Nevertheless it is clear that some record of this warning, as well as of the warning in legal form, should be kept, so that, ". . . its execution can be established."[69] On this point it should be immediately noted that the Sacred Congregation for Bishops and Regulars on September 7, 1801 ordered that paternal warnings should not be filed in the public records of the episcopal chancery. It provided instead, that some memorandum of the issuance of such a warning should be kept in the secret archives.[70] This measure is taken to protect the good name of the person who is corrected. At the same time it serves the twofold purpose of a reference in the event that further steps must be taken later against the same person, and in case the Bishop is requested by higher authority to give an accounting for his action.[71]

66 *Sacra Haec*, n. 6: . . . aut per interpositam personam. . . .

67 Lega, *Praelectiones*, IV, 355, n. 285.

68 *Canonical Procedure*, p. 150.

69 *Sacra Haec*, n. 6: . . . ita tamen ut de earumdem executione constet ex aliquo actu.

70 *Analecta Iuris Pontifici*, XX (1881), p. 82.

71 Cf. *Sacra Haec*, n. 5.

b. *In Forma Legali*

The canonical warning given in legal form deals generally with the same matters as the paternal and secret warning. It, too, is chiefly concerned with the obligations of state in life. It includes both the correct fulfilling of various duties and the avoiding of certain stimuli of scandal and proximate occasions of delicts.[72]

As has been previously stated, the warning which is given in legal form utilizes the presence of witnesses. For the most part, this warning thus parallels the pattern of fraternal correction as outlined in the Gospel text, "But if he do not listen to thee, take with thee one or two more so that on the word of two or three witnesses every word may be confirmed." [73]

This pattern cannot be taken, however, as the only one to be followed. Lega states that a form is legal or apt for proof if the chancellor includes a text of the warning in the *acta* of a case, or if witnesses are used and may testify that a warning was given, or else when the Bishop presents a written copy of the text of the warning and requires the signature of the person to whom the warning is given.[74] Thus while the Gospel pattern may be frequently employed, the use of witnesses for a warning in legal form may also include the ecclesiastical notary, or the combined testimony of the Ordinary and the person being warned who, by his signature, may himself be a witness to the fact that a warning was given.

Apparently the use of witnesses serves several purposes: (1) The solemnity produced by the presence of legal witnesses is calculated to impress the person who is corrected with the seriousness of the matter and to arouse him with greater force to recover his senses and adjust his conduct.[75] (2) If he nevertheless refuses to heed the warning, the witnesses will give manifest proof that it was made, and their testimony will serve as evidence in a judicial procedure.[76] Thus a warning in legal form is one which is judicially acceptable

[72] *Sacra Haec*, n. 2.

[73] St. Matthew, 18, 16.

[74] *Praelectiones*, IV, 355, n. 286.

[75] Cf. Messmer, *Canonical Procedure*, p. 151.

[76] Cf. Lega, *Praelectiones*, IV, 355, n. 286.

as a vehicle upon which to construct a trial if such a necessity arises.

By reason of these features, the warning in legal form is seen to be more severe than the paternal and secret warning. Lega concurs with this view and concludes that the intention as well as the nature of these two types of warning is such that it may be easily inferred that one should follow the other, i. e. the paternal warning should be given first and then followed by the legel warning, if this is necessary.[77] He realizes, however, that sometimes the subject matter and the circumstances of a particular case are of such a nature that the Ordinary judges the paternal warning to be useless because it would be ineffective. In these cases the Ordinary is expected to by-pass the lesser warning and proceed immediately to give a warning in legal form.[78]

Because of its more severe nature, the warning given in legal form requires more grave indications of guilt than were required for the paternal warning. The summary investigation of the facts still need not reveal full proof, however. Lega notes that the warning in legal form is especially useful when an investigation reveals less than full proof, but the proof which is uncovered is of such a nature that it urgently moves the Bishop to employ penal measures.[79]

In the same fashion as the paternal warning, the one given in legal form may also be delivered personally by the Ordinary meeting face-to-face with the person being warned. If the Ordinary prefers another method, the warning may also be given by letter or through an intermediary.[80] When given by letter, it should be done by a formal document, i. e. signed by the chancellor or other ecclesiastical notary and not by a private secretary.[81]

Ordinarily all warnings which are given in legal form should be filed in the public records of the chancery office.[82] It may frequently happen, however, that they may better be deposited in the

[77] *Praelectiones*, IV, 356, n. 287.

[78] *Ibid.*

[79] *Praelectiones*, IV, 357, n. 287.

[80] *Sacra Haec*, n. 6.

[81] Messmer, *Canonical Procedure*, p. 151.

[82] Lega, *Praelectiones*, IV, 356, n. 286.

secret archives instead of the public files because of the persons, the subject-matter or the circumstances which are involved. In this way greater precaution is taken to protect the person's good name; and at the same time, the possibility of notoriety and subsequent *admiratio populi* or even scandal may be reduced. For clerics, this use of the secret archives may be a means of preserving their reputation so that they may still be able to perform their sacred ministeries in an effective manner.[83] Messmer observes that while warnings are public in so far as they become known to the law, they frequently must be kept secret from the public.[84] Among other cases which may be cited as examples when the secret archives should be used, would be the warnings which are given for occult crimes. Since no one should be punished publicly for an occult crime, all warnings in relation to such crimes should likewise be kept secret.

c. *Scholion. Warnings and the Threat of Penalty*

A final point which may be considered in relation to both the warnings *in forma paterna et secreta* and *in forma legali* is whether or not they may or should contain a threat of a punishment. There are several divergent opinions on this matter.

In his treatment of the penal remedies, Wernz presents the position that paternal warnings are given without penal sanction,[85] and that canonical warnings are the same as penal precepts.[86]

This view hardly seems tenable when articles nn. 6 and 7 of *Sacra Haec* are compared. In article 6 of the Instruction, both of the warnings *in forma paterna et secreta* and *in forma legali* are listed as canonical warnings. Both are apparently to be considered and spoken of as canonical warnings. It is then stated in article 7 that if these warnings fail or are fruitless, then a corresponding precept in kind, containing a threat of an ecclesiastical penalty, is to be enjoined upon the person. Thus it seems that the precept is distinct from the warnings and is to be used only after the warnings *in forma paterna et secreta* and *in forma legali* have been found

83 Lega, *loc. cit.*

84 *Canonical Procedure*, p. 151.

85 *Ius Decretalium*, VI, 261, n. 255.

86 *Op. cit.*, p. 260, n. 255.

to be fruitless. The Instruction makes no provision for the warnings to contain a threat of a punishment; whereas it explicitly prescribes that the precept should contain a specific threat of a penalty. Thus, the position of Wernz to the effect that paternal warnings contain no threat of punishment, but that canonical warnings are the same as precepts and therefore contain a threat of a penalty, does not seem to be in accord with *Sacra Haec*.

Lega's position is proximate to, but different from, that of Wernz.[87] He believes that a warning may, and frequently should, contain a threat of a penalty. On the other hand he realizes that the lack of full and legitimate proof would hinder the including of a threatened penalty with a paternal warning. In like manner he observes that the Bishop should refrain from threatening *latae sententiae* penalties in any paternal warning because he would be unable to produce a legitimate decree upon which to base a declaratory sentence. He believes, however, that a canonical warning in legal form, by its very nature, calls for a penal sanction upon the contumacious who would spern the authority of the Bishop as he gives an exhorting and salutary warning. Nevertheless he realizes that prudence and charity often urge that a warning be given in legal form, but without the accompanying threat of a penal sanction.

Lega looks more to the Instruction for his opinion than Wernz does. It is true that the nature of the warnings is such that oftentimes they precede the more severe remedies and punishments for those persons who remain stubborn and contumacious. In this sense the warnings by their very nature threaten a penalty implicitly upon the person corrected. It is difficult to see, however, how it can be concluded that the warnings may contain an explicit threat of a penalty. Since Lega believes that sometimes the threat of penalty may be omitted by reason of prudence and charity, it seems that he also holds that at other times the warnings may include a threat of penalty. As was observed above, the Instruction contains no specification for the inclusion of a threat of penalty in the canonical warnings,[88] as is clearly specified for the precept.[89]

Messmer holds the view that both types of warnings are "mere

87 Cf. *Praelectiones*, IV, 356, n. 286.

88 Cf. *Sacra Haec*, n. 6.

89 *Sacra Haec*, n. 7.

correction and reproof."[90] For this reason he believes that no matter how severe or strong their wording or manner of delivery might be, the warnings should not contain a threat of punishment. It is his opinion that such threat of punishment should be restricted to the canonical precept.

The present writer subscribes to the view of Messmer, for this seems to comprehend the mind of the Instruction. From *Sacra Haec* it is clear that the precept must contain a threat of a penalty. It is clear also that since different names were given to them, the warnings are not intended to be the same as the precept. Otherwise only warnings or precepts would indiscriminately have been prescribed to do the task of all the preservative remedies. There seems to be a definite difference between the canonical warnings and the precept, and one basis for this apparent difference would be the absence or presence of a specific threat of an ecclesiastical penalty.

3. THE PRECEPT

When the warnings prove to be fruitless, the Ordinary should instruct his curia to impose a precept about the matter upon the delinquent. This precept should clearly indicate what is to be done or omitted and should be accompanied with the threat of an ecclesiastical penalty which the delinquent will incur in case he transgresses the precept.[91]

Thus, the Ordinary issues a command to the person being corrected, making it clear to him exactly what is expected of him, and making this command equally clear by including the threat of an ecclesiastical penalty in case of his disobelience. As can be readily seen, this remedy is much more grave than either of the warnings. While not indicated in the Instruction, Messmer notes that it is to be used when the warnings have been to no avail, or when the Ordinary finds them to be fruitless by judging the temperament of the delinquent, the circumstances of the offense, etc.[92]

The Instruction refers to an "analogous precept."[93] This termi-

[90] *Canonical Procedure,* p. 151.

[91] *Sacra Haec,* n. 7.

[92] *Canonical Procedure,* p. 152.

[93] *Sacra Haec,* n. 7.

nology is understood to mean that the subject-matter (i. e. the delicts or dangers of evil) is the same as that which occasioned the warnings or would have been the subject-matter of the warnings if they had been given.[94]

There is no specification in *Sacra Haec* as to what type or types of ecclesiastical penalties could be threatened in the penal precept. While it is Messmer's position that, "this punishment, however, is always *ferendae sententiae*," [95] there seems to be nothing in the text of the Instruction to verify this position. Certainly the *ferendae sententiae* penalty would very frequently be the most desirable one in the mind of the Church and the most likely one to be imposed. For particularly grave cases, or situations where only an *ipso facto* penalty would seem to be an adequate deterrent, there is no reason why a *latae sententiae* penalty could not be threatened for disobedience of the precept.

The formalities to be observed in issuing the canonical precept are prescribed in some detail [96] and may be summarized as: (1) Citation of the delinquent to appear for the precept; (2) The precept is read to the delinquent by the chancellor in the presence of the Vicar General or two witnesses; (3) Signing of the *Acta* in witness thereof [to be filed in the chancery]; (4) Oath of secrecy, if advisable.

The fact that the person to be corrected is officially cited to appear at a definite time to hear the precept is not specifically stated. It is clearly deduced, however, from the fact envisioned in the context, that the person (the *praeventus*) is present at the issuance of the precept.[97]

Once the *praeventus* has appeared, the precept is to be given to him or read to him by the chancellor in the presence of either the Vicar General or two ecclesiastical or lay witnesses of proven integrity. Messmer adds that the precept must be drawn up in writing and contain the name of the Ordinary in whose name it is being issued, the name of the person to whom it is issued, the clear indication of what is to be done or omitted, and the threat of the

94 *Canonical Procedure*, p. 152, note 2.

95 *Canonical Procedure*, p. 152.

96 *Sacra Haec*, n. 8.

97 *Ibid.*

ecclesiastical penalty which will result from disobedience to the precept.[98]

A time limit for its observance may be established in the precept itself, otherwise the lapse of a reasonable length of time for amendment or further correction before the penalty would be inflicted would be left to the prudent judgment of the Ordinary.

Following the giving of the precept before the witnesses, the document containing the precept is signed by all persons who are officially present and also by the person receiving the precept if he so wishes.[99] As in the case of the warnings, this record is to be filed in the chancery archives.[100]

If the circumstances of the case would demand it, and it seems that most often they would, the Vical General may impose an oath to observe secrecy about these transactions and this subject upon those present.[101]

4. PENAL MEASURES

Next the Instruction directs its attention to "penal measures."[102] While not expressly stated, this term seems definitely to refer to the repressive remedies mentioned in article n. 2.[103] *Sacra Haec* reminds Ordinaries that in the application of "penal measures" the solemn judicial procedure may be continued wherever this can be freely and efficaciously employed. The summary or economical form is permitted where the cases or the curias are such that the solemn form is impossible or not expedient to be used. These "penal measures" are thus identified as those remedies which may be inflicted after a solemn or summary judicial process, and are seen to refer to the repressive remedies.[104]

98 *Canonical Procedure*, p. 154.

99 Cf. *Sacra Haec*, n. 8, § 1.

100 *Canonical Procedure*, p. 154.

101 *Sacra Haec*, n. 8, § 2.

102 *Sacra Haec*, n. 9.

103 This identity becomes more apparent when one examines a corresponding provision of *Cum Magnopere* and finds that the repressive remedies (*remedia repressiva seu poenas*) are expressly treated in n. 9 of this latter Instruction of 1883.

104 As a special warning in the use of penal measures, it is pointed out

The remainder of *Sacra Haec* is concerned with instituting and executing the new summary procedure and is not of immediate interest to this present study.

Article III. The Instruction *Cum Magnopere*

Just three years after the appearance of *Sacra Haec*, the Sacred Congregation for the Propagation of the Faith issued a similar Instruction *Cum Magnopere*[105] for the handling of disciplinary and criminal cases of clerics in the United States of America. This action was calculated to solve the problems which had developed in the Church in this country, where the rapid multiplication of dioceses could not always be accompanied with the establishment of a curia and tribunal fully staffed; and where the zealous, if impatient, spirit could not always submit to the minutiae of the solemn legal procedure. The existing legislation, coupled with some rule-of-thumb private interpretations of these laws, had resulted in disharmony rather than order in the young and growing Church. The Instruction *Quamvis* of July 20, 1878, to the United States[106] had not fulfilled its intended goal of remedying the situation. Rather it produced doubts of its own, and responses to these doubts led in turn only to further doubts and misunderstandings.

Most often when there is lack of uniform understanding and

that in no place is there to be an altering of the prescripts of the Council of Trent regarding the use of the extra-judicial remedy *ex informata conscientia* for handling occult crimes.—Cf. Conc. Trident., sess. XIV, *de ref.*, c. 1.

105 S. C. de Prop. Fide, instr., a. 1883—*Fontes*, n. 4900; *Collectanea*, n. 1586.

106 Cf. *Acta Sanctae Sedis* (41 vols., Romae, 1865-1908), XII (1879), 88-92. This Instruction provided for a commission of three or five priests to be appointed in each diocese, with the chief function of aiding the Bishop in his examination of the criminal and disciplinary causes of clerics by making an accurate investigation into the matter. Recognizing that the full judicial procedure could not always be observed in the United States, provisions were hereby made that at least an accurate investigation into the crime would be made before a penalty could be inflicted. While being concerned with all ecclesiastical punishments for clerics, the Instruction made a special effort to correct the inept removal of missionary rectors from their offices. In substance, this investigation was not a judicial process, but was a form of administrative procedure.

application of law in any society, there will result the two-fold effect both of injustice to some individuals and a lessening of respect for the authority of those who are applying the law. This result was the condition of the Church in the United States in 1883, and this is what the Sacred Congregation for the Propagation of the Faith set out to correct.

The Instruction *Cum Magnopere* was issued, as its Introduction testifies, for the avowed purpose of providing for ecclesiastical trials of such a nature that their manner of procedure would be adapted to the wants of the times as well as be adequate for the regular administration of justice. At the same time it sought to protect the authority of Prelates and stop the cause of complaints [of injustice] on the part of the accused.[107]

Thus issued with the approval of Pope Leo XIII [1878-1903], the Instruction abrogated the previous legislation of 1878 and the responses thereto except for those things which were retained in the new Instruction. *Cum Magnopere* adequately provided for a uniform system of procedure for the disciplinary and criminal causes of clerics in the United States. As uniform as possible, at least, in view of the fact that some of the dioceses were still so new and understaffed that they temporarily lacked the necessary organization and clerical assistance to comply completely with the Instruction.[108]

As far as their application in the United States is concerned, there is a great difference between the Instructions *Sacra Haec* and *Cum Magnopere*. *Sacra Haec* was for Italy and possibly Europe as a whole, but it had no direct bearing on disciplinary matters in the United States of America. *Cum Magnopere,* on the other hand, was issued for the United States. It applied to every diocese where it was possible to put it into effect.

As for their contents, however, the general treatment of the subject matter of both Instructions follows an identical pattern. *Cum Magnopere* is almost an exact copy or transcript of *Sacra*

107 Cf. *Cum Magnopere,* Introductio.

108 Provision was made for this contingency in n. XII. By papal dispensation those dioceses in which an episcopal curia could not as yet be established were, in the meantime, to follow the Instruction of 1878 and the subsequent responses related to it.

Haec. The few variations in their texts may indicate some slight development of concept in the later legislation, but seem mostly to be due to an effort to achieve greater clarity of expression.

A few differences between *Cum Magnopere* and the previous *Sacra Haec* which may be noted are as follows:

1. It is unequivocally stated that the preventive remedies are especially spiritual exercises, warnings and precepts.[109]

2. Greater emphasis is given to the secret aspect of the canonical warning, rather than its paternal aspect. Reference is made to canonical warnings given *secreto . . . ad modum paternae correptionis.*[110]

3. The term, "repressive remedies" is used as being equivalent to the term "penalties."[111] Apparently the repressive remedies are used only after a delict has been committed and the delinquent has been identified. This conclusion would imply that he has either confessed or has been found guilty.[112]

4. Unlike *Sacra Haec* this Instruction does not state that the older solemn formalities of judicial procedure may well be followed when this is possible.

109 *Cum Magnopere,* n. IV.

110 *Cum Magnopere,* n. VI. The present writer believes that this approach in describing the secret warning, is an attempt to extricate this canonical entity from any confusion of identity with a merely paternal or charitable warning and admonition. The emphasis is directed, therefore, to differentiate between warnings in secret and those given in legal form, rather than between paternal and legal. Thus this presentation is much clearer than the concept produced by *Sacra Haec* (n. VI.) with its terminology of, ". . . *in forma paterna et secreta.*"

111 *Cum Magnopere,* n. IX.

112 The Instruction makes it clear that the usual system concerning repressive remedies is not to be employed when there is a matter involving the Tridentine process of *suspensio ex informata conscientia* in occult cases, i. e. there are to be no judicial proceedings before the remedy is imposed. In line with this, Smith observes, "A canonical trial or *processus judicialis* must precede all repressive punishments, save in the case of suspension *ex informata conscientia.*"—Smith, *New Procedure in Criminal and Disciplinary Causes of Ecclesiastics in the United States* (2. ed., New York: Fr. Pustet & Co., 1888), 20 [hereafter cited *New Procedure*].

Article IV. The Legislation of the Third Plenary Council of Baltimore

The provisions of *Cum Magnopere* were readily accepted and applied by the hierarchy of the United States. Within a short time they were even slightly reenforced by enactments of further particular law for this country established in the Third Plenary Council of Baltimore in 1884.[113]

The general pattern of thought in the provisions of this Council is the same as embodied in the Instruction of 1883—the milder remedies are to precede the more grave; and only after both have been proven to be ineffective, should the Bishop resort to a judicial process and more severe ecclesiastical penalties. The remedies to be employed are: the paternal warning, the canonical warning and the precept.

In its legislation the Council added a few qualifications and amplifications to the text of *Cum Magnopere*:

1. The preliminary summary inquiry into the facts is looked upon as an *Inquisitio,* which could be either general (where the existence of an abuse or a delict but not the name of the offender is brought to the attention of the Bishop) or special (where both the existence of the abuse or delict and the identity of the offender are made known to the bishop).

2. If witnesses are interviewed in the preliminary inquiry, this must be done secretly, and they must be heard privately i. e. one at a time.

3. Along with the paternal warning an opportunity must be given to the suspected cleric to offer a defense against the accusation or matter of suspicion. He must also be given the opportunity to agree to a reform and thus avoid the need for further disciplinary action.

4. If the paternal warnings are fruitless, then the canonical warnings are to be used, observing the legal form.[114]

[113] Cf. Conc. Pl. Balt. III., nn. 308-310—*Acta et Decreta,* p. 176-178.

[114] Here it seems that the Council of Baltimore equates secret with paternal form, and canonical with legal form. This, as has been seen, was not the sense of either Instruction.—Cf. *Sacra Haec,* n. 6, *Cum Magnopere,* n. VI. Both secret and legal form warnings are classified as canonical.

5. Three canonical warnings may be given over a period of six days, i. e. two days should elapse between warnings.

Besides the above particularizations, the Council reemphasized the fact that, except for the extra-judicial repressive remedy *ex informata conscientia,* no repressive penalty ought to be used unless there had been a previous judicial process or at least a summary process where that method is permitted.

Thus within the brief span of four years the concept and method of application of the canonical remedies was presented by *Sacra Haec* (1880), applied to the United States by *Cum Magnopere* (1883), and slightly specified further as particular law for the United States of America by the Third Plenary Council of Baltimore (1884).

CHAPTER II

THE CHARACTERISTICS AND DEFINITION OF THE PENAL REMEDIES OF THE CODE

The Code of Canon Law clearly prescribes the use of the penal remedies as one of the measures which may be employed to curtail the activity of deliquents in the Church.[1] By this fact these remedies are given canonical status and are constituted as one of the official methods of ecclesiastical punishment.[2]

Likewise the Code presents a list of these remedies [3] and indicates the occasions on which they may be used, who may give them, the interrelation of one remedy with another, the manner in which they are to be or may be imposed (secret, public), and the mode which is employed in imposing them publicly (judicial, extrajudicial).[4] At no place, however, does the Code give a definition of the penal remedies.

In the absence of an official definition, therefore, it seems of immediate importance, for usefulness if not absolute necessity, to establish one before proceeding. This may well serve the twofold purpose of: presenting a comprehensive over-all concept of the penal remedies (one of the objectives of this dissertation), and formulating a definition of the penal remedies as they are employed in the Church today (an objective of this chapter).

Article I. A Definition of the Penal Remedies, Derived From Their Concept and Characteristics as Contained in the Pre-Code Law

The concepts expressed in the Instruction *Sacra Haec* are still suitable for consideration in the establishment of a definition of the penal remedies to the extent that their application is still in

1 Cf. c. 2216.

2 This is substantiated by the rubric of Book V, Title IV: *De poenarum notione, speciebus, interpretatione atque applicatione.*

3 C. 2306.

4 Cc. 2307-2311; 1933, § 4; 1946; 1947-1953; 2223; 2224; 2234.

force in the Code.[5] Even though they are not given expressly as a definition in the Instruction, for the present these concepts may well be treated as such here. The penal remedies may thus be defined as: CANONICAL REMEDIES USED TO PREVENT AND ELIMINATE DISTURBANCES OF THE SOCIAL ORDER.[6]

This general definition of penal remedies seems acceptable for the following reasons:

1. They are *canonical* because they are prescribed by the canons as an expression of the coercive power of the Church, which is ". . . native and proper to the Church, independent of any human authority."[7]

2. They are *remedies* because they strive to keep the Church as a society and its individual members in a state of spiritual well-being. They also seek to remedy the undesired effects of overly harsh or inadequate penalties.

3. They *prevent* and *eliminate* because these are the specific functions of the two types of penal remedies—a) preventive, and b) repressive and corrective.[8] They strive to stamp out evil which is grave enough to be a delict either by preventing an impending evil or by eliminating one which already exists.

4. They are concerned with *disturbances of the social order* because their objective is to maintain order in the external forum so that the Church as a perfect society will be able to fulfill Her God-given purpose, the sanctification and salvation of mankind.

While being correct, this definition still lacks several elements which characterize and further particularize the penal remedies. For these it seems that one may do well to draw upon the provisions of the Council of Trent. The thirteenth session of this Council, as has been seen in the preceding chapter, urges Bishops, as good shepherds, to apply *mild anodynes* to the disorders of their flocks before proceeding to the use of the sharper and more severe remedies.[9] Whether or not this measure was intended by the

5 C. 6, 2°-3°.

6 Cf. *Sacra Haec*, n. 1.

7 C. 2214, § 1.

8 *Sacra Haec*, n. 2.

9 Conc. Trident., sess. XIII *de ref.*, c. 1.

Fathers of the Council to be an implicit recommendation and forerunner for the use of the penal remedies is of no immediate concern at this time. The fact is that the penal remedies have come to be an actual realization and fulfillment of this objective expressed by Trent—the use of mild means against disorders among the flock, before employing the more severe measures; and the application of this discipline so that the rest of the flock might be protected.

Another characteristic which is noteworthy in the legislation of this Council is that Trent recommends a much wider application of these mild remedies. *Sacra Haec* (and *Cum Magnopere*) applied canonical remedies only to the clergy, whereas Trent looked to their use among all who were subject to the Bishop. This latter provision is also in keeping with the Code, which gives no indication that the penal remedies are only to be used in respect to the clergy.

Thus from the Council of Trent three elements of the definition may be adopted: Penal Remedies are: (1) MILD REMEDIES; (2) TO CORRECT DISORDERS COMMITTED BY ECCLESIASTICAL SUBJECTS; (3) TO PROTECT THE REST OF THE FLOCK FROM THE DANGER OF CONTAGION.

Finally, from both Trent and *Sacra Haec* there is a property which is not to be so taken for granted that it is overlooked. It is the BISHOP OR LOCAL ORDINARY WHO HAS THE POWER TO IMPOSE THESE REMEDIES.

From the concepts inaugurated by the Council of Trent and the Instruction *Sacra Haec,* therefore, the penal remedies may be defined as:

> **Mild canonical remedies imposed by the Bishop upon persons subject to his authority, to prevent and eliminate disturbances of order within the society of the Church.**

ARTICLE II. A DEFINITION OF THE PENAL REMEDIES, DERIVED FROM THIER CONCEPT AND CHARACTERISTICS AS CONTAINED IN THE CODE OF CANON LAW

An examination of the Code of Canon Law reveals that it continues the general concept of the pre-Code canonical remedies in the penal remedies of the Code, and presents the latter with even greater clarity and broader application. Besides indicating an extension of their use, the present legislation still reveals characteristics of how, when, why, by whom, and to whom the penal remedies are to be applied.

While keeping in mind the concepts which have been retained from the pre-Code law, some characteristics of the penal remedies of the Code may be given further consideration and emphasis at this point.

SECTION A. MODERATION

1. MODERATION—A TRADITION OF CHURCH DISCIPLINE

The administration of justice through moderation rather than severity has found place among the finest traditions of the Church. To claim this, is not to say that there were no exceptions, or even that in some periods of history it was the general norm. The abuse and non-use of moderation is a matter of record. The fact, however, that the hierarchy, assembled in synods and councils,[10] passed disciplinary canons against the arbitrary or servere administration of justice, itself attests that they were conscientiously striving to correct the element of harshness along with the other abuses of their day, reminding their erring confreres of their duties in the role of shepherds, not persecutors, of their flock.[11] These councils, therefore, point not only to the abuses but also to the fact that the compassion of Christ, not severity, was to be the traditional measuring rod in the administration of justice by the Church. Obliged all the while to protect itself and its members from contamination and disturbances of its social order, the Church strives with reserved self-control to effect a mild yet ever-firm and adequate discipline over the faithful.

Since their relative mildness is one of the chief particularizing characteristics of the penal remedies of the Code of Canon Law, it would be well to examine a bit more closely the claim that moderation is a traditional attribute in the discipline of the Church.

Gratian ascribes to St. Jerome (340[?]-420) the apt observation:

---

10 E.g. III Council of Carthage (397), c. 38—Bruns, *Canones Apostolorum et Conciliorum Saeculorum* IV-VII, (2 vols., Berolini, 1839) I, 128 [hereafter cited Bruns]; III Council of Braga (675), c. 7—Bruns, II, 100.

11 Cf. Conc. Trident., sess. XIII, *de ref.*, c. 1.

> . . . For good rectors are mindful of the infirmities of others from their own weakness, and strive to assist them rather through humility and clemency, trying to snatch sinners from the trap of error, than through austerity to hasten those who are tottering into the pitfall of perdition.[12]

Thus, while an Ordinary, by reason of his office, must correct the abuses and evils of his flock, he must at the same time be a student of human nature and be mindful of the human weaknesses of his subjects. He must not excuse evil on the gounds that he also is weak; for the duty of his office demands otherwise. But humility and clemency will have an influence on his manner of correcting. In this he follows well the traditional pattern of St. Paul, who became weak to those who were weak [13] in his efforts to persuade the early Christians to follow Christ more closely.

The Roman Pontiffs have given ample witness of the existence of moderation as a characteristic in the exercise of the coercive power of the Church. Among others, one might cite Pope Leo I and Pope Gregory I.

Pope Leo I [440-461] in a letter to Anastasius, Bishop of Thessalonica, writes that the bishop must be on his guard against a compromise in his duty to correct, resulting from either flattery which inflates his pride, or from a peace-at-any-price attitude. He adds, however, that although being obliged to correct erring members of the clergy, he must be mindful that ". . . kindness is better than severity, exhortations better than emotional outbursts, charity better than a show of power." [14]

In a commentary on one of the letters of Pope Leo I,[15] Joannes Teutonicus [† 1245] explains that a Bishop's learning must be extended to two fields: to the discipline of correction and to

[12] C. 16, D. XLV.

[13] I Corinthians, 9, 22.

[14] Epist. LXXXII (circa 446)—Jaffé, *Regesta Pontificum Romanorum ab condita Ecclesia ad annum post Christum natum MCXCVIII* (2 ed., *correctam et auctam auspiciis* Guglielmi Wattenbach, *curaverunt* F. Kaltenbrunner [for documents up to the year 590], P. Ewald [for documents from 590 to 882], S. Lowenfeld [for documents from 882 to 1198], 2 vols., Lipsiae, 1885-1888) n. 411; c. 6, D. XLV [hereafter cited Jaffé].

[15] *Epist. ad Septimum Aquilegensi* (442) [Bishop Septimus of Aquileja] —Jaffé, n. 398.

preaching the word of God. By way of explanation, he adds that a Bishop must be learned in the art of giving discipline so that ". . . he might correct in a spirit of charity and leniency and not through hate or with excess in his methods of correction." [16] Likewise, in his letter to Rusticus, Bishop of Narbonne, Pope Leo I counsels that there should be ". . . hatred for sins, not men; the proud should be corrected, the weak sustained; and when it is necessary to give a more severe correction, it should be done with the spirit of a physician. . . ." [17]

Pope Gregory I [590-604] also testifies to the tradition of the use of moderation. A strong example may be cited from his letter to Bishop John of Constantinople, written in 593:

> . . . That view which develops faith by force is unheard of and an innovation, for we are shepherds, not persecutors. The distinguished preacher [St. Paul] says, 'reprove, entreat, rebuke with all patience and teaching.' [18]

In his letter to all the Bishops of Gaul, Germany and throughout Europe, he also emphasizes the fact that in administering correction, kindness is better than severity, exhortation better han an emotional outburst, charity better than a show of power.[19] Then he recalls the charitable and understanding Christ Who forgave St. Peter even after his three-fold denial, and intimates that they are to act in like manner. He closes his letter with words that may be considered the "Golden Rule" for those administering justice and discipline, and which present the traditional pattern: ". . . he should not dare to treat others in a manner in which he would not wish to be treated himself." [20]

Again in his tract on morality, the Pontiff speaks of the part which both firmness and clemency share in the administration of discipline. He points out that there is a complete inter-dependence

[16] *Glossa ordinaria*, ad c. 1, D. LXXXVI, *Decretum Gratiani, emendatum et notationibus illustratum una cum glossis* (Romae, 1583).

[17] Leo I, Letter to Rusticus, Bishop of Narbonne, Epist. CLXVII (458-459)—Jaffé, n. 544; c. 2, D. LXXXVI.

[18] Gregory I, Letter to John, Bishop of Constantinople (593)—Jaffé, n. 1257; c. 1, D. XLV; II Timothy, 4, 2.

[19] Letter of Gregory I (590-604)—Jaffé, n. 2579.

[20] *Ibid.*

between the one and the other: ". . . each depends so much upon the other that there is neither a strength which is unbending, nor a clemency which is mere unfruitful weakness."[21] For this reason, discipline should not be imposed without mercy, nor mercy without discipline. At another place in the same tract, Pope Gregory I reiterates this inter-dependence and association which must exist between correction and mildness. He insists that firm discipline and mildness must be partners in correction, and he cites the parable of the Good Samaritan to fortify his position. The man who had been beaten by robbers and left to die was restored to health through the combined use of both wine and oil upon his wounds [22]—wine to stop infection, oil to heal. It was the combination of these two which restored the man to health. The same may be said for firmness and mildness.

The use of moderate measures in the interest of justice and equity is not a characteristic merely of the traditions of other centuries. Indeed, it has not ceased to be employed, but rather plays an integral part in the discipline of the Church today. As evidence that moderation has its place in the ecclesiastical legislation of today, one may advert to the address of the Most Reverend Amleto [now Cardinal] Giovanni Cicognani, D. D., given to The Cannon Law Society of America.[23] This timely address, by the then Apostolic Delegate to the United States, considered the topic *Canonical Equity and the Salvation of Souls,* and looked both to the past and to current legislation in the Code to beautifully portray the Church fulfilling Its role as the Good Shepherd of souls.

After quoting St. John Chrysostom to the effect that, 'Justice without mercy is not justice, but cruelty; just as mercy without justice is foolishness," His Excellency inferred that Christian equity developed from the Church's effort to achieve fairness and modera-

[21] Gregory I, *Moralium,* lib. XIX, cap. 20, n. 30—*Migne, Patrologia Cursus Completus, Series Latina (221 vols., Parisiis, 1844-1864)*, LXXVI, 118 [hereafter cited *MPL*].

[22] Gregory I, *Moralium,* lib. XX, cap. 5—*MPL,* LXXVI, 143; c. 9, D. XLV.

[23] Address at the Twentieth Annual Meeting of The Canon Law Society of America, Washington, D. C.: Mayflower Hotel, October 15, 1958.—Cf. *The Jurist,* XIX (1959), pp. 1-11.

tion in Its discipline. In recalling numerous apt examples of the spirit of canonical equity which permeates the Code, the Penal Law of the Church received generous attention; and the use of moderation, tolerance, restraint, and great circumspection in the application of penalties was cited as being the mind of the Church. In concluding his lucid presentation, His Excellency observed:

> . . . You are ministers of justice and goodness. In approaching any problem, you have to apply the law without rigid severity and without harmful laxity. However, you must bear in mind that the purpose of the law is to promote the salvation of souls, and you should employ to the fullest extent canonical equity and the juridical institutions available to you. Conforming to the mind of the Church, which is the Mind of Christ, the Saviour, with the aid and guidance of Canon Law, you are to assist in the pastoral work of helping men to secure the possession of the truth and grace of Christ, and to live and die in holiness, piety and fidelity to the Church. . . .

While delivered to the assembled members and guests of The Canon Law Society of America, these thoughts also encompass all who are burdened with the responsibility of exercising the coercive power of the Church. Being of universal application, this address gives an excellent testimony that moderation is not only a legislative tradition of the past centuries of the Church, but also has place in the discipline of the Church today.

2. MODERATION—A CHARTERISTIC OF THE PENAL REMEDIES

One of the particularizing characteristics of the penal remedies is their definite mildness. As such, they are a fine example of moderation in Church legislation as considered above. This mildness of the penal remedies is, of course, a relative quality—they are mild in relation to the ecclesiastical penalties of suspension, interdict, deprivation of benefice, degradation of clerics, excommunication, etc.; they are not mild when compared to the absence of any disciplinary action at all. The legislator intends this comparative mildness of the penal remedies. Indeed, their quality of mildness is a notable modern testimony of the Church's desire and continued earnest attempt to administer justice in as humane a manner as possible. It is justice tempered with mercy, a glowing example of equity.

With the hope that, in consideration of the circumstances involved, they will be adequate for their purpose, the penal remedies are used to protect the social order of the Church by employing the appropriate remedy at the proper time. They seek, in part, to remedy an unhealthy situation without having to resort to the more grave methods of punishment. Sipos points out this design by observing that when penal remedies are used to prevent the commission of delicts and they are effective, the public order is kept from being greatly violated and, all the while, the more grave method of criminal trial does not have to be applied.[24]

While preventing or repressing an abuse, they may nevertheless protect and preserve the honor and good name of a member who has imprudently endangered it by his wicked or suspected delictual conduct. At times their moderation is likewise a means of avoiding any disturbance of the social order which could result from *admiratio populi* if a more serious penalty were applied and the heretofore secret occasion of the penalty became public knowledge.

Smith[25] observes that it is readily admissible that sometimes there are weighty reasons for not prosecuting a criminal or not inflicting an ecclesiastical penalty at all. This forbearance is understandable when consideration is given to the fact that at times the penalty might cause more harm than good to the person corrected by leading him to despair rather than causing him to amend. Again, such disciplinary measures might have the undesirable effect of implicating and harming the honor and good name of a third party. In these cases, too, the relative mildness of the penal remedies offers a solution to the problem both in the interest of justice and the parties involved.

Within the penal remedies themselves there is also a definite relativity in degrees of mildness and severity. Thus c. 2306 presents a hierarchy among the remedies ranging from the warning to surveillance: the mildest is the warning; surveillance is the most severe. While surveillance is the least mild of the penal remedies, it is nonetheless considered to be a mild punishment when compared to the medicinal and vindictive penalties of the Code.

[24] Sipos, *Enchiridion Iuris Canonici* (Rome: Herder, 1954), p. 852 [hereafter cited *Enchiridion*].

[25] *New Procedure*, p. 27.

In view of this gradation of relative mildness among the penal remedies, it is thought that the Ordinary should employ the mildest which he prudently judges will be adequate to prevent or correct a particular situation.[26] Roelker concurs with this view and states: "Apparently the remedies mentioned in canon 2306 are not to be used indiscriminately, but gradually, according to their need."[27]

SECTION B. CANONICAL MEASURES

1. CANONICAL

The first reason for considering the penal remedies to be canonical is the fact that they are prescribed by the sacred canons. They are included in the Code's enumeration of official methods of ecclesiastical discipline and punishment.[28]

Over and above the listing of these remedies in the Code of Canon Law, the authors[29] point to another basis for their canonical aspect. To these experts the penal remedies are considered to be canonical because they are expressions of the coercive power of the Church in the external forum so that the Church may accomplish its purpose as a society.

Lega defines canonical as being that which is employed by the power of a public authority of the Church.[30] DeMeester concurs with this concept of Lega, and notes also that the warning is called canonical because it proceeds from the public authority of an Ordinary.[31]

Likewise, in speaking of the warning as a penal remedy, Sipos points out that the matter in question deals with a canonical warning. He explains that this term refers to that which is issued

26 Cf. Blat, *Commentarium*, V, 190, n. 143; This is also in accord with the provisions of *Sacra Haec*, n. 3; and *Cum Magnopere*, n. III.

27 Roelker, *Precepts* (Paterson: St. Anthony Guild Press, 1955), p. 194 [hereafter cited *Precepts*].

28 Cf. c. 2216: In Ecclesia delinquentes plectuntur . . . Remediis poenalibus. . . .

29 E. g. Lega, DeMeester, Sipos, Vermeersch-Creusen.

30 Cf. *Praelectiones*, IV, 353, n. 284.

31 *Compendium*, p. 228, n. 1802.

by a Superior through his power of jurisdiction, and not to a paternal warning which is issued by a Superior without using his penal power.[32] He thus equates the term canonical with the concept of that which is issued by reason of a Superior's power of jurisdiction.

Vermeersch-Creusen have a similar view, and state that a canonical warning is one which is given by a Superior or by a judge, based upon jurisdiction, in order to stop or prevent an act.[33] It is upon this definition that they draw specific attention to the nature of a secret warning, and point out that this is a canonical and not a paternal warning, properly so-called. They note that a paternal warning is that which is given by a Superior as the moral leader of an imperfect society, based upon dominative power, especially and primarily intended for the improvement of the individual; whereas a canonical warning as has been stated, comes from someone having jurisdiction and seeks to correct the act itself.[34] They further note that a distinction may be made between a paternal warning and a canonical warning given *in forma paterna*; and conclude that the Code clearly does not deal with paternal warning when treating the penal remedies.[35] The penal remedy of warning is thus seen to be canonical even when it may be given *in forma paterna.*

It is reasonable to presume that what has been said of the term *canonical* in relation to the warning, may similarly be accepted for the other penal remedies. Thus the penal remedies are canonical because: (1) they are prescribed as punishments in the Church by the sacred canons; and (2) they are employed by an authority of the Church having the exercise of jurisdiction in the external forum.

2. MEASURES

Although the penal remedies differ among themselves in so far as each one has its own specific properties and conditions for

[32] *Enchiridion,* p. 852.

[33] Vermeersch-Creusen, *Epitome Iuris Canonici* (6. ed., Rome, 1946), III, 307, n. 502 [hereafter cited *Epitome*].

[34] *Loc. cit.*

[35] *Epitome,* III, 308, n. 503.

application, they nevertheless, both singly and as a group, have the common characteristic of being means to an end. They are not desirable as objectives in themselves, but are rather one of the groups of methods, tools or vehicles through whose agency the social order in the Church is protected and maintained.

The fact that the penal remedies are *means* to the achieving of an objective is noted by Coronata,[36] Vermeersch-Creusen,[37] and Sipos.[38] Coronata also alludes to them as penal *norms* in so far as they possess in some manner and degree the nature of penalty.[39]

On the other hand, Ayrinhac-Lydon use the term *measures* to describe the penal remedies in their treatment of Title X of the Code, noting that the penal remedies are, ". . . certain *measures* taken by the ecclesiastical authority to prevent the occurence of evil. . . ."[40]

While both terms, *norms* and *means*, are readily admitted to be very apt descriptions for the penal remedies, the present writer has a preference for the use of the term *measures*. This preference is based on the opinion that *measures* seems to contain a shade more of reference to the dynamic quality of active correction and prevention which is not possessed by the other terms. The English word *norm* seems to have a more static quality and would be better employed to describe a standard or rule of conduct. While the term *means* certainly describes the characteristic of the penal remedies used as instrumentalities for a specific course of action, it

36 Coronata, *Institutiones Iuris Canonici* (4. ed., 5 vols., Romae: Marietti, 1955), IV, 79, n. 1689: ". . . They are preventive *means* to obstruct more serious delicts . . ." [hereafter cited *Institutiones*]. [Italics and translation supplied by the present writer.]

37 *Epitome*, III, 306, n. 501: "Penal remedies are *means* used by a competent superior to remove the faithful from the occasion of a delict . . ." [Italics and translation supplied by the present writer]

38 *Enchiridion*, p. 852: "Penal remedies are certain penal *means* of preventing delicts, which anticipate delicts or at least check them lest public order is greatly violated . . ." [Italics and translation supplied by the present writer]

39 *Institutiones*, IV, 281, n. 1838.

40 Ayrinhac-Lydon, *Penal Legislation in the New Code of Canon Law* (revised ed., New York: Benziger Bros., 1936), p. 134, n. 176 [hereafter cited *Penal Legislation*].

nevertheless does not seem to admit the idea of correction and prevention as strongly and aptly as the word *measures* does.

Section C. The Preventive Aspect of Penal Remedies

It may be said that in one manner or other all use of coercive power in the Church has the objective of deterring the faithful from crime and protecting the society of the Church by preventing the commission of delicts.[41] The penal remedies, however, have this preventive characteristic to the extent that it is considered to be their essential and particularizing trait.[42] Indeed, whenever the penal remedies are employed, a property which is always present, and in most cases emphasized, is this crime-prevention aspect. To make this statement is not to deny the repressive value of the penal remedies, but to acknowledge the part which the preventive characteristic plays in their over-all makeup.

In their role of crime-prevention, the penal remedies are used to comprehend a present situation in its relationship to the future. Their purpose is thus to forestall an approaching evil so that the stimuli of scandal, the voluntary occasions and the proximate causes of delinquency may be removed.[43] As crime-preventives the remedies may be used subsequent to the fact that a delict has already been committed,[44] and in this case they try to prevent the continuance or future repetition of the delict. On the other hand, some of the penal remedies, the warning and the precept, may also be used even before an actual delict has been committed,[45] or where

[41] Cf. Beste, *Introductio In Codicem* (4. ed., Neapoli: D'Auria Pontificius Editor, 1956), p. 960 [hereafter cited *Introductio*].

[42] Cf. Coronata, *Institutiones*, IV, 79, n. 1689.

[43] Cf. c. 2307; *Sacra Haec*, n. 2; *Cum Magnopere*, n. II. From another point of view, the penal remedies are also preventive. Whenever they are effective in accomplishing this purpose, there is usually no need for the Ordinary subsequently to have to resort to the more severe types of punishments. As long as the penal remedies are efficaciously received, therefore, they prevent the necessity of inflicting greater punishments.

[44] Cf. cc. 1933, § 4; 1947-1953; 2223, § 3, 3°; 2224, § 2; 2309, § 3; 2310; 2225; 2234.

[45] C. 2307 prescribes that the warning may be issued to someone who is merely "... in proxima occasione delictum committendi ..."; and canon 2310 states that the precept should be used in the same case when

there is no absolute proof of the existence of a delict, but where the investigation produces a grave suspicion that a delict has been committed.[46] In these latter uses, the remedies of warning and precept are employed to prevent the commission of the first delict or the continuation of a probable delict.

In all of their uses the least common denominator for all penal remedies is their preventive characteristic. This aspect may at times have an objective which is simply preventive, and at other times it may be preventive-repressive. In every case these remedies strive to preserve order in the society of the Church by preventing both progression into crime and the need of resorting to greater punishment.

The preventive characteristic of the penal remedies thus affords a fine example of the solicitude and benignity of the legislator and his efforts to protect the Church in as mild, yet all the while as efficacious, an exercise of coactive power as possible. Here is an attempt to strike at the roots and beginnings of evil. As such, it typifies the constant warfare between the forces of good and evil which accompany daily living. Here also one finds God's Church engaged in its unrelenting fight against evil, yet administering justice tempered with the charity of Christ.

The authors who treat of the subject are unanimous in calling attention to the penal remedies as preventive measures. Their views merit our attention and may be summarized here.

DeMeester notes this characteristic when he states that for the good of the faithful, penal remedies are used in order to avoid a delict [*ad vitandum delictum*].[47]

Sipos likewise refers to the preventive aspect of the penal remedies by observing that they are certain penal means of preventing delicts, which anticipate the delicts or at least check them lest public order is greatly violated. It is his expressed view that they are preventive means because they preserve from serious delicts.[48]

the warning was found not to be effective, or where it was judged useless even to give the warning.

46 According to canon 2307 the warning may be issued to someone "... in quem ex inquisitione peracta, gravis suspicio cadit delicti commissi ..."; and canon 2310 provides that the precept may be used in the same case also.

47 *Compendium*, p. 139, n. 1708, *ad* c. 2216.

48 *Enchiridion*, p. 852.

Vermeersch-Creusen at least implicitly allude also to the preventive nature of the penal remedies when they note that they are means used by a competent superior to remove the faithful from the occasion of a delict or to check a grave fault while it still lacks the proportions of a delict.[49]

Roelker cites Chelodi to the effect that penal remedies are given to prevent crime rather than to punish it.[50]

Ayrinhac-Lydon maintain the same opinion and incorporate the concepts of the Instruction of 1880 into their statement that the penal remedies are certain measures taken by the ecclesiastical authority to prevent the occurrence of evil, forestall scandal, remove voluntary occasions and all proximate causes of delinquency.[51] They add that the penal remedies may also be considered as preventive punishments because they aim to prevent, rather than chastise, wrong-doing.[52]

Wernz, in his discussion of the Instruction *Sacra Haec,* also notes that the preventive remedies receive their name from the fact that they protect against the commission of grave delicts.[53]

Coronata calls attention to the fact that the penal remedies are used to complete a criminal trial and also to supplement or increase a penalty, but he emphasizes that they are given especially in order to prevent delicts.[54]

Besides the opinions of the authors listed above, it may be recalled here that in the Instruction of 1883, two of the penal remedies which are now in the Code were singled out as being especially useful as preventive remedies. These were the warning and the precept.[55] Spiritual exercises were also in this list, but now are included in the Code not as penal remedies but rather as penances.[56]

49 Vermeersch-Creusen, *Epitome,* III, 306, n. 501.

50 Roelker, *Precepts,* p. 192; Chelodi, *Ius Poenale* (Tridentini, 1935), p. 71.

51 *Penal Legislation,* p. 134, n. 176.

52 *Ibid.*

53 *Ius Decretalium,* VI, 258, n. 253.

54 *Institutiones,* IV, 281, n. 1838.

55 Cf. *Cum Magnopere,* n. IV.

56 Cf. c. 2313, § 1, 5°.

Benefits Derived From Using Preventive Remedies

There can be little doubt that the penal legislation of any society is more perfect if it is able, with apt penalties and measures, to prevent its subjects from committing delicts. Wernz praises this aspect of the penal law of any society and notes that by such preservative action the society is freed from disturbances of its order.[57] By the existence of these preventive means, there is no need of waiting until harm has been done to a community before its cause is corrected. The society is thus spared the existence of many delicts and scandals. In the use of the penal remedies, the Church thus takes a prompt and firm stand against any grave external evil which has the potentiality of interfering with Its function and progress as a society. By the use of these remedies, delicts, and even cases involving suspected or potential delicts, are attacked before they are allowed to occupy an entrenched position and seriously disrupt the order among the faithful.

The preventive measures are likewise more agreeable to the Ordinary who must impose them, for they afford him a better method to fulfill his duty. Without such measures at his disposal the Ordinary would be obliged to resort to juridically weaker and inadequate methods of correction or else wait until the delict had been committed before adequate steps to protect the faithful could be taken. With these canonical measures he can suppress potential abuses oftentimes before they become an actuality. The Ordinary may thus better fulfill his duty as shepherd of his flock. At the same time these equip the Ordinary with an equitable instrument of justice, and yet give him the possible means of avoiding the very distasteful task of issuing the more severe types of punishment.

For the person receiving the preventive remedy there also seems to be a great advantage and benefit. These give him an opportunity to correct a fault or salvage a spiritually unhealthy situation before the stigma of crushing penalties is laid upon him.

The preventive characteristic of the penal remedies, therefore, whenever in practice it proves to be adequate to meet the needs of a particular situation, gives the penal legislation of the Code

57 Cf. *Ius Decretalium*, VI, 258, n. 253.

a quality which is better for the society of the Church, better for the Ordinary, and better for the person being corrected. For everyone concerned then, it is a very useful aspect of discipline and correction.

Section D. The Preventive-Repressive Aspect of Penal Remedies

1. Repressive Remedies in General

The term *repressive remedies* has frequently been used to refer to canonical *penalties*. As such it is a broad generic term. Indeed the Instruction of the Sacred Congregation for the Propagation of the Faith issued in 1883 uses the terms *repressive remedies* and *penalties* as synonyms.[58] In like manner, the Third Plenary Council of Baltimore (1884) utilizes the same concept in its terminology.[59]

In his excellent book on Precepts, Roelker remarks, "If the remedies used in the exercise of coactive power be divided into preventive and repressive remedies, as is done, for instance, in the Instruction of the Sacred Congregation for the Propagation of the Faith, the former will be considered penal remedies and the latter penalties." [60]

In both the pre-Code and post-Code eras then, the repressive remedies are considered to be penalties which are imposed upon someone who has been found guilty of a delict, by extra-judicial means, formal trial, or the Tridentine process *ex informata conscientia.*[61] These strive to effect a return to moral good health and well-being in cases where a delict has already been comitted, and they seek to recall the delinquent to the point that he will regain his wisdom and balance of values and consequently repair the evil effects of his crimes.[62]

[58] *Cum Magnopere*, n. IX: . . . remedia repressiva seu poenas. . . .

[59] *Acta et decreta*, n. 310: . . . ad remedia repressiva seu poenas pertinens. . . .

[60] *Precepts*, p. 192.

[61] Smith, New Procedure, p. 38; *Acta et decreta* III C. Balt., n. 310; *Cum Magnopere*, n. IX.

[62] Cf. *Sacra Haec*, n. 2 .

2. PENAL REMEDIES AS REPRESSIVE REMEDIES

In the Code, a function for the penal remedies is indicated which so qualifies their nature that they too, must be considered as a species of the repressive remedies, though not necessarily one of the true ecclesiastical penalties.[63] The function of the penal remedies now is not only that of a preventive remedy, as intimated by Roelker, but over and above this consideration they have a definite use in the Code as a repressive remedy also. Coronata draws attention to this fact when he states that it is evident that the Code has extended and, in some measure, changed the notion of penal remedies as given before the Code.[64] He cites the use of the judicial rebuke by the Ordinary for the purpose of avoiding a criminal trial.[65] He may just as well have referred to the other instances when the penal remedies are employed in such a manner that their function, while not necessarily excluding the preventive objective, is that of one of the repressive remedies. The following uses of the penal remedies may be so cited:

1. The penal remedies are used as substitutes for a *poena determinata* when the circumstances of the case call for a mitigation of the penalty.[66]

2. When the judge employs the penal remedies in addition to a severe penalty in cases where the plurality of penalties actually incurred by the delinquent for a number of delicts would make the deserved sentence unbearable.[67]

3. When surveillance or other penal remedies may be added to a penalty in order to increase it because of the plurality of the delicts which were committed.[68]

63 There is no intention here to consider the characteristic of penality which is possessed by the penal remedies. Nor is there any attempt to consider these remedies in their relationship to the medicinal and vindictive penalties. Both of these aspects will be treated in Chapter III. The only topic of immediate attention is that while the penal remedies are preventive remedies, the Code also employs them at times as repressive remedies as well.

64 *Institutiones*, IV, 281, n. 1838 footnote.

65 C. 1947 considered with c. 2309, §§ 3, 4.

66 C. 2223, § 3, 3°.

67 C. 2224, § 2.

68 C. 2234.

In the above cases the penal remedies are employed as repressive remedies. A delict is not considered as impending, but rather as having already been committed. The delinquent has either confessed or has been found guilty. The remedy is used at least partially to bring the erring member back to a sense of duty and to repair the evil effects of his misdeeds.[69]

Berutti cites this aspect of the penal remedies and states that one of their objectives is the correction and reform of someone who either has already committed a delict or is in the danger or occasion of committing a delict. Thus he says: "They are either to prevent or to repress abuses." [70]

It may be noted here that Roelker also alludes to a use for the penal remedies which is other than preventive. He states that, "While the purpose of a precept as a penal remedy is preventive, as indicated in the Instruction of the Sacred Congregation [for Bishops and Regulars] its actual use may go beyond mere prevention of crime." [71]

In accord with the citations from the Code and the opinions expressed above, it is clear that the penal remedies may be included among the categories of both the preventive and repressive remedies. A comprehensive definition of the penal remedies must, therefore, refer to both of these characteristics.

3. PENAL REMEDIES ARE PREVENTIVE-REPRESSIVE

To speak of their repressive function is not to de-emphasize the role of the penal remedies as preventive measures. Indeed it seems evident that their preventive and repressive aspects are by no means mutually exclusive, but rather may, and frequently do, co-exist. This result occurs in cases where the delinquent has confessed or has been convicted of a crime.[72] When the penal remedies are employed in such cases, they may be repressive in regard to the present crime, and preventive in regard to the possibility of committing future crimes. They are repressive in so far as they are

[69] These are the objectives of the repressive remedies as stated in *Sacra Haec*, n. 2 and *Cum Magnopere*, n. II.

[70] *Institutiones*, VI, 63.

[71] *Precepts*, p. 194.

[72] E. g. cc. 2309, § 3; 1947; 2223, § 3, 3°; 2224, § 2; 2234.

intended to recall the delinquent to his sense of duty and to repair the consequences of his crimes. At the same time they may be preventive because they proposed to prevent the occurrence of future evils, forestall scandal and remove the voluntary occasions and proximate causes of the delinquency.

Roelker is aware of this aspect of the precept as a penal remedy and observes: "A precept, then, considered in this way is not a preventive penal remedy except in regard to future crimes. As a penal remedy more important than correction, the precept can be considered equivalent to a condemnatory sentence." He concludes, however, that this is not the principal function of a precept as a penal remedy.[73] He thus points to the fact that a penal remedy may simultaneously be employed in a case both as repressive of present evil and preventive for future crimes.

When one realizes that the penal remedies may be used when a delict has already been committed, and yet that the purpose of their use is at least partially to prevent or deter the commission of future delicts, it seems that all penal remedies, even those which are represessive, contain some preventive element. Therefore, when the repressive element of the definition is considered, it seems best described as preventive-repressive.

Beste sums up this characteristic by stating that the primary scope of the penal remedies is the prevention of crimes, but secondarily they participate also in the nature and purpose of the repressive penalties.[74]

Section E. Types of Cases Specified by Law for Application of the Penal Remedies

This section is intended to present briefly the various types of cases for which the penal remedies are prescribed by the Code.

Although their ultimate objective is always to maintain the social order of the Church, these preventive and preventive-repressive measures may be employed in various ways. Depending upon a variety of circumstances, the penal remedies may be legitimately used as follows:

---

[73] *Precepts*, p. 195.

[74] Cf. *Introductio*, p. 1021.

1. To prevent the commission of a delict when someone is in the proximate occasion of falling into crime.[75]

2. To properly warn someone upon whom the grave suspicion of delinquency remains after an investigation of the matter has been made.[76]

3. To correct a frequent manner of conduct which has been the cause of scandal or grave disturbance of order.[77]

4. To substitute for a penalty when a penal remedy is considered to serve adequately against someone who has confessed or has been convicted of a delict.[78]

5. To mitigate a *poena determinata* when there is indication that circumstances have notably lessened the imputability for the delict; or when the delinquent either has apparently reformed, or has already been punished by the civil authority.[79]

6. To mitigate the penalty in the interest of reasonableness and equity, when the accumulation of penalties due for a number of delicts committed would seem unbearable.[80]

7. To increase a penalty when several delicts have been committed.[81]

8. To impose the penalty of surveillance if the delinquent is judged to be in the danger of lapsing into the same crime.[82]

Thus, the law provides for a variety of wise and useful applications of the penal remedies. Special attention will be given to some of these in chapter four, where canons 2306-2311 will be considered in detail.

Section F. Imposition by a Competent Authority

Who may impose the penal remedies? The Code contains explicit mention of the ecclesiastical authorities who are to employ these

[75] C. 2307.

[76] C. 2307.

[77] C. 2308.

[78] C. 2309, §§ 3, 4; c. 1947-1953.

[79] C. 2223, § 3, 3°.

[80] C. 2224, § 2.

[81] C. 2234; 2309, § 4.

[82] C. 2311, § 1.

disciplinary and corrective measures. From these explicit provisions of the Code, it may also be deduced that all other superiors and officials of the Church are implicitly excluded from the number of those persons who may resort to the penal remedies in the exercise of their respective authority and offices. In the event of a valid doubt whether or not a certain superior shares this power, the presumption would favor a negative answer to the advantage of the one subject to disciplinary correction (*in poenis benignior est interpretatio facienda*).[83]

The Code clearly provides that the penal remedies may be imposed by the Ordinary when he is acting either judicially or extra-judicially [84] (exclusive of the Vicar General without special mandate),[85] by the Judge of the curia when he is exercising his judicial power at a trial,[86] and by a Superior [87] competent to impose at least a jurisdictional precept.[88] These are the only ones to whom the Code gives the authority to impose a penal remedy.

1. THE ORDINARY

The Instructions *Sacra Haec* and *Cum Magnopere* both provided that the application of the canonical remedies was to be left to the conscience of the Ordinary.[89] These same provisions have substantially been continued in the Code.[90] Canon 2307 gives the Ordinary the task of issuing the warning,[91] and canon 2308 deals

83 C. 2219, § 1.

84 Cf. cc. 2307-2311.

85 C. 2220, § 1.

86 Cf. cc. 2309, § 3; 2223, § 3, 3°; 2224, § 2; 2234.

87 C. 2309, § 6.

88 C. 2220, § 1.

89 Cf. *Sacra Haec*, n. 3: Conscientiae et prudentiae Ordinarii horum remediorum incumbit applicatio juxta canonum praescriptiones . . . ; *Cum Magnopere*, n. III: Conscientiae Ordinarii remittitur cujusque remedii applicatio, canonicis praescriptionibus servatis pro casuum ac circumstantiarum gravitate.

90 Cf. Blat, *Commentarium Textus Codicis Iuris Canonici* (5 vols., Romae: Typographia Pontificia in Instituto Pii IX, 1924), V, 190, n. 143 [hereafter cited *Commentarium*].

91 Ordinarius per se vel per interpositam personam moneat.

with his delivery of the rebuke.[92] Canon 2310 provides that whenever the warning and the rebuke have been found ineffective or are considered to be useless, then the precept is to be given the subject. While the Ordinary is not specified in this canon as the author of the precept, it is reasonable to hold that he is the one who is competent to issue a precept as a penal remedy. This position is in accord with canon 2220, § 1, which provides that whoever has the power to make laws or impose precepts is able also to fortify the observance of his laws or precepts by attaching a penal sanction for disobedience to them.[93] As a complement to this consideration, canon 2214, § 1 stipulates the existence of coercive power in the Church, and canon 2214, § 2 indicates that this authority is possessed by [local] Bishops and other Ordinaries,[94] who should act as true shepherds of their flocks. Furthermore, since the use of the precept as a remedy is mentioned both in the Code and in pre-Code legislation, the present law must be understood according to the interpretation of the former legislation.[95] The former law, exemplified by both of the Instructions *Sacra Haec* and *Cum Magnopere,* explicitly specified that it was the Ordinary who was to give the precept when the canonical warnings had failed or were found to be fruitless in a particular case.[96] It seems clear, therefore, that the precept as a penal remedy may be imposed by an Ordinary.

Finally, canon 2311, § 1 specifies that the Ordinary is to be the one who imposes the remedy of surveillance upon a delinquent.[97]

Who then is the Ordinary? In law, unless otherwise expressly excluded, the term Ordinary includes the Roman Pontiff for the

[92] . . . est locus correptioni, ab Ordinario per se vel per interpositam personam, etiam per epistolam faciendae. . . .

[93] C. 2220, § 1: Qui pollent potestate leges ferendi vel praecepta imponendi, possunt quoque legi vel praecepto poenas adnectere.

[94] Meminerint Episcopi aliique Ordinarii se pastores non percussores esse. . . .

[95] C. 6, 2°-4°.

[96] *Sacra Haec,* n. 6: Quatenus infructuosae monitiones evadant, Ordinarius praecipit curiae, ut delinquenti analogum iniungatur praeceptum . . . ; *Cum Magnopere,* n. VI: Quod si monitiones in irritum cedant, Ordinarius jubet, per curiam delinquenti analogum praeceptum intimari . . .

[97] C. 2311, § 1: . . . eum Ordinarius submittat vigilantiae.

whole Church, the residential Bishop, Abbot *Nullius,* Prelate *Nullius,* together with their Vicars General, and also the Apostolic Administrator, Vicar Apostolic, and Prefect Apostolic, each for their own proper territories. It likewise includes those who by prescript of law or approved constitutions would succeed to the administration of these offices during the interim caused by the incapacity of the previous incumbents; and Major Superiors of exempt clerical religious institutes for their own subjects.[98]

a. *Vicar General Excluded*

When there is a question of which of these Ordinaries may impose penalties, one must be mindful of the express provisions of canon 2220, § 2. In the light of this canon, the Vicar General does not have the power to inflict penalties unless he has received a special mandate to do so.[99] The term *poenas* in this canon apparently must be understood to mean ecclesiastical punishments in the broad sense rather than ecclesiastical penalty in the strict sense of canon 2215.[100] This interpretation would be in accord with the benign interpretation prescribed by the Code, because it would thereby limit the number of persons who may impose ecclesiastical punishments upon a delinquent.[101] In regard to the use of the penal remedies, therefore, none of them, even those which may not comprise all of the requirements of a true penalty of canon 2215, could be imposed by the Vicar General unless he had a special mandate from his residential Ordinary to do so.

The authors are in accord in stating that the Vicar General is excluded from the ranks of those Ordinaries who may impose the penal remedies. In commenting on the phrase *Ordinarius per se vel per interprositam personam* as referred to the warning,[102] Jone states that the title *Ordinary* as used here does not include the

[98] C. 198, § 1.

[99] Vicarius Generalis sine mandato speciali non habet potestatem infligendi poenas.

[100] Poena ecclesiastica est privatio alicuius boni ad delinquentis correctionem et delicti punitionem a legitime auctoritate inflicta.

[101] C. 2219: In poenis benignior est interpretatio facienda.

[102] C. 2307.

Vicar General because of the prescriptions of canon 2220, § 2.[103] He makes the same statement regarding the judicial rebuke of canon 1947[104] and the precept of canon 2310.[105] Coronata and Sipos makes similar observations to the effect that the warning cannot be given by the Vicar General without a special mandate, and they base their reasoning on canon 2220, § 2.[106] Augustine likewise explains the term *Ordinary,* as used in relation to the warning and rebuke, to signify " the diocesan bishop or the prelate *nullius* or the exempt religious superior, but not the vicar-general, unless he has received a special commission for this purpose. The reason is that penal remedies partake of the nature of penalties, concerning which, according to canon 2220, § 2, the vicar-general is not competent in virtue of his office."[107] Vermeersch-Creusen say that the Vicar General needs a special mandate to inflict the judicial rebuke because canon 2309, § 4 indicates that it is issued in place of a penalty and it is employed to punish for the commission of a delict.[108] In regard to the precept of canon 2310, they likewise note that the Vicar General cannot add a threat of an ecclesiastical penalty without a special mandate. Their position is also based on canon 2220, § 2.[109] Similarly Cocchi states that the precept should be imposed by the Ordinary, excluding the Vicar General unless he has a special mandate as prescribed by canon 2220, §2.[110]

Although none of the authors seem to deal with the possibility of the Vicar General inflicting the remedy of surveillance, it is reasonable to presume that, since this is the " severest of the penal

[103] Jone, *Commentarium in Codicem Iuris Canonici* (3 vols., Paderborn: F. Schöningh, 1955), III, 491 [hereafter cited *Commentarium*].

[104] *Op. cit.*, p. 270.

[105] *Op. cit.*, p. 493.

[106] Coronata, *Institutiones*, IV, 284, n. 1841; Sipos, *Enchiridion*, p. 853.

[107] Augustine, *A Commentary on the New Code of Canon Law* (2. ed., 8 vols., St. Louis: B. Herder Co., 1924), VIII, 268 [hereafter cited *Commentary*].

[108] *Epitome*, III, 139, n. 267.

[109] *Epitome*, III, 309, n. 504.

[110] *Commentarium*, VIII, 210, n. 124.

remedies," [111] he would need a special mandate for this remedy also. Canon 2220, § 2 could, of course, also be the basis for this position.

It should be noted here that, while the imposition of the penal remedies must originate with an Ordinary other than the Vicar General unless he has a special mandate, the latter may serve as the *interpositam personam* spoken of in canons 2307 and 2308. Jone [112] and Augustine [113] both remark that along with the rural dean and the pastor, the Vicar General would be a fine choice to act in the capacity of intermediary between the Ordinary and the person being subjected to the penal remedy.[114]

Having established the position of the Vicar General in relation to the penal remedies, the other Ordinaries may now be considered in the remainder of this section.

b. *All Other Ordinaries Included*

The Roman Pontiff, of course, enjoys the supreme and full power of jurisdiction throughout the universal Church both in matters of faith and morals and in those matters which deal with the discipline and regulation of the Church spread thoughout the world.[115] This power exercised by His Holiness is truly episcopal, ordinary and immediate in its application to each and every Church, and each and every official and member of the faithful.[116] Whenever the occasion would require it, therefore, the Pope may impose the penal remedies upon any member of the Church.

What of the other Ordinaries? Roelker quotes Ottaviani to the effect that by reason of the constitution of the Church, a residential Bishop possesses legislative power and that radically this power is found in his office.[117] It is clear that after a Bishop has been canonically appointed by the Roman Pontiff [118] and has taken

111 Augustine, *Commentary*, VIII, 270.

112 *Commentarium*, p. 491.

113 *Commentary*, VIII, 268.

114 When a remedy is thus issued by the Ordinary through the mediation of a third party the rule of law is employed: *Potest quis per alium, quod potest facere per seipsum*—Reg. 68, R. J. in VI°.

115 C. 218, § 1.

116 C. 218, § 2.

117 Cf. Roelker, *Precepts*, p. 42.

118 C. 332.

canonical possession of his diocese,[119] he has the right and the office of governing his diocese in both spiritual and temporal matters with legislative, judicial and coactive power according to the norms of the sacred canons.[120] Provided no limitation has been placed on him by higher ecclesiastical authority, the residential Bishop can use this power to meet all the demands of fulfilling the obligations of his office. By reason of this jurisdiction attached to his office, then, the residential Bishop is empowered to govern with authority and is definitely set apart from the subjects whom he governs. Roelker states that this power is not merely a directive or persuasive faculty, but a ". . . superiority which finds its roots in the very nature of the Church itself." [121] The superior-subject relationship which accompanies the residential Bishop's office enables the Bishop to enact laws or impose precepts with equal obligation of obedience; and because he thereby shares in the exercise of the coactive power of the Church, he may fortify his legislation with apt penal sanctions.[122] Among the other exercises of authority over his subjects, the residential Bishop may also employ the penal remedies upon those who require his correction.

Unless the Holy See has made some reservation of power in a particular situation, the Vicar Apostolic and the Prefect Apostolic enjoy the same rights and faculties in their respective territories as the residential Bishop does in his diocese.[123]

The same may also be said for the Apostolic Administrator if his letter of appointment does not restrict his jurisdiction, and he is established permanently in his position.[124] If his appointment is only temporary, then his status is similar to that of a Vicar Capitular.[125] While this latter status is expressly restricted by provisions of law in respect to the performance of many administrative acts,[126] there is no additional limitation placed upon his

[119] C. 334, § 2.

[120] C. 335, § 1.

[121] Cf. *Precepts*, p. 44.

[122] C. 2220, § 1.

[123] C. 294.

[124] C. 315, § 1.

[125] C. 315, § 2, 1°.

[126] Cf. cc. 357, § 1; 373, § 5; 406, § 1; 454, § 3; 492, § 1; 686, § 4; 893, § 1; 1303, § 3; 1423, § 1; 1487, § 1; 1500.

exercise of coactive power. In either a permanent or a temporary appointment, therefore, the Apostolic Administrator would enjoy the same power in regard to discipline and ecclesiastical punishments as is afforded the residential Bishop by reason of his office. In case the Apostolic Administrator is sent to a See which is not vacant, and the letter of appointment has not placed any limits upon his exercise of jurisdiction, then the jurisdiction of the incumbent residential Bishop will be suspended for the duration of the Administrator's term.[127]

The Abbot *Nullius* and the Prelate *Nullius* likewise have the same ordinary powers and obligations as the residential Bishop in his own diocese.[128]

When a residential See is vacant, the Cathedral Chapter,[129] or the Diocesan Consultors in those countries where there is no Cathedral Chapter,[130] receive the ordinary jurisdiction of the Bishop in temporal and spiritual matters, except for those things which are expressly prohibited by law.[131] Within eight days these must in turn appoint a Vicar Capitular. Once the Vicar Capitular has taken the profession of faith prescribed by canons 1406-1408, he immediately receives the same ordinary jurisdiction[132] of the [residential] Bishop in both temporal and spiritual matters, except in those things expressly prohibited by law.[133] As has been noted above in the discussion of the Apostolic Administrator, no specific limitation is made by law upon the coactive power of the Vicar Capitular.

All of the above Ordinaries, therefore, by reason of their office in the Church enjoy the exercise of coactive power and may issue penal remedies. The basis for their action has foundation in the existence of coactive power in the Church.[134]

The Major Superior of an exempt clerical religious Institute is

127 C. 314; c. 316, § 1.

128 C. 323, § 1.

129 C. 431, § 1.

130 C. 427. Such is the case at present in the United States of America.

131 C. 435, § 1.

132 C. 432, § 1; c. 438.

133 C. 435.

134 Cf. Roelker, *Precepts*, p. 192.

also classified as an Ordinary in regard to his own subjects.[135] It is clear that he may impose ecclesiastical penalties of the Code upon his subjects unless a particular penalty has been withdrawn from his competency by particular law or by the Holy See. It must be noted here that this power is not possessed by all superiors of religious Institutes, even Major Superiors, but is limited to Major Superiors of exempt clerical religious Institutes.

There seems to be no immediate import to this discussion to consider why some superiors are classified as Ordinaries and others are not. It is a matter of legal fact that although a religious superior has no radical power in the constitution of the Church, nevertheless some superiors have been given the status of Ordinaries by the Holy See.[136] Since the Code provides that the penal remedies are to be issued by Ordinaries, these Superiors are thus qualified also.

[135] C. 198, § 1.

[136] Roelker notes that: ". . . a religious superior has no radical power in the constitution of the Church. Whatever relationship exists between such a superior and his subject is fundamentally and essentially a contract, real or implied, within the limits of the constitution of the religious society. That a real relationship exists is evident from the presence of the elements of a real society. From such a relationship certainly arises a power to command by some kind of precept; but from this relationship would not essentially arise the power to impose *jurisdictional precepts.* This would require additional power which can be granted only according to the provisions of the constitution of the Church. Therefore, a jurisdictional precept, in the exact sense in which a bishop can impose such a precept, is possible to a religious superior only by concession of the Pope and not by contribution of subjects in religious communities nor by custom or prescription. Some religious superiors enjoy this concession of the Pope; others do not."—*Precepts,* pp. 42-43.

What is said here about the jurisdictional precept is also applicable to the precept as a penal remedy of the Code of Canon Law and the other ecclesiastical punishments. If specific superiors possess the power to impose them upon anyone, it is not by reason of the vows or promises of their subjects, but by concession from a source which has this power, viz., the Holy See.

Roelker is mindful, however, that other superiors may impose penalties upon their subjects, which penalties, while not identical with them, are *analogous* to ecclesiastical jurisdictional penalties. He states that: "The penal precepts of Superiors possessing only dominative power cannot threaten or impose ecclesiastical penalties. . . . As Schaefer points out,

This power to impose ecclesiastical penalties is possessed by all who are included in the term Major Superior: the Abbot-Primate, the Abbot Superior of a monastic congregation, the Abbot of an independent monastery even though it forms part of a monastic congregation, the Supreme Moderator and Provincial Superior of Religious Institutes together with their vicars and all others who have the powers equivalent to those of Provincials.[137] When these are Superiors of an exempt clerical religious institute, they may issue penal remedies to those who are subject to their authority.

it is not contrary to canonical principles, however, for the higher Superiors and the chapters of congregations and societies where dominative power exists to institute certain penalties which in an *analogous* sense are called vindictive penalties and which would punish certain determined crimes. . . . Wernz-Vidal limit the coactive power of Superiors possessing only dominative power to the milder forms of spiritual and temporal penalties. The vigilance of the superiors must concern itself with the observance of the constitutions, domestic discipline, and the progress toward perfection; and in order to obtain proper attention to these items, penal precepts can be imposed."

"The doctrine of Schaefer and Wernz is thoroughly in keeping with the notion of dominative power. No member of a society, by submitting himself to the authority of a Superior by promise or vow, surrenders more than is contained in such a promise or vow. If further power exists, it is the concession of the Church which transfers the exercise of jurisdiction to specific Superiors"—Roelker, *Precepts*, pp. 175-176.

Since only the Major Superiors of exempt clerical religious institutes are classified as Ordinaries by the Code, the Superiors of the other religious institutes in the Church cannot be considered as Ordinaries. Consequently these Superiors who are not Ordinaries do not share in the authority to impose ecclesiastical punishments as Ordinaries do.

It is the opinion of the present writer that when Religious Superiors who are not Ordinaries properly exercise the authority given them by their respective constitutions and employ the warning, rebuke, precept, or surveillance, they are using remedies which are *analogous* to the penal remedies of the Code. These analogous remedies do not, however, have the same canonical status of ecclesiastical punishments as the penal remedies of the Code of Canon Law.

137 C. 488, 8°. Creusen-Ellis note that: "In many institutes the first assistant or the first councillor of a superior general exercises supreme authority when the superior general is absent or impeded or has resigned, as also during the interval between the death of a superior general and the election of his successor. Does it necessarily follow that the first assistant or first councillor is a major superior? A distinction must be

2. THE JUDGE

In every diocese for all those cases which are not expressly withdrawn from his competency, the local Ordinary is the judge of first instance.[138] He may exercise his judicial power and, as the judge, impose penal remedies to substitute for a *poena determinata,*[139] to modify a penalty,[140] or to complement a penalty.[141] Likewise, in the case of a public rebuke, the Ordinary is said to act judicially when before a criminal trial he issues the rebuke as a penalty to someone who has confessed his guilt.[142]

The local Ordinary can also exercise his judicial power *per alios* according to the prescripts of the sacred canons.[143] For this purpose every residential Bishop is obliged to appoint an *Officialis,* who constitutes one tribunal with the local Ordinary.[144] By this act of appointment, the judicial power of the residential Bishop is communicated to the diocesan judge through the bestowal of his office.[145] Thus while the Bishop may personally preside over his tribunal in all cases in which he is competent, he is strongly urged to leave the criminal and contentious judicial proceedings of a serious nature to the *Officialis* or *Vice-Officialis.*[146]

According to the Code, the judge is to employ the penal remedies only when he is actually sitting in tribunal.[147] When he gives a

made here. When he actually takes the place of the superior general he has the powers of a major superior; outside such times his office does not carry any authority with it unless the constitutions or the superior general entrusts him with the care of certain persons or of certain matters of business."

"The term *vicar* is employed instead of "provincial" in certain institutes better to indicate dependence upon the superior general and unity of government."—*Religious Men and Women in the Code* (5. ed., Milwaukee: Bruce, 1953), p. 18.

138 C. 1572.

139 C. 2223, § 3, 3°.

140 C. 2224, § 2.

141 C. 2234.

142 C. 2309, § 3; c. 1947-1953.

143 C. 1572, § 1.

144 C. 1573, § 1, § 2.

145 Cf. Roelker, *Precepts,* p. 125.

146 C. 1578.

147 C. 2309, § 3; 2223, § 3, 3°; 2224; 2234.

judicial rebuke, Jone notes that the judge does this at the end of the process because c. 2309, § 4 states that such a rebuke is given in place of a penalty or to increase a penalty.[148] The judge may not give the judicial rebuke, however, when the delinquent confesses his guilt before the actual formal trial has begun.[149] It seems also that the Ordinary, but not the judge, may issue a judicial rebuke after the trial has begun but before the case has been completed.[150]

3. THE SUPERIOR

Besides the Ordinary and the judge who actually forms one tribunal with the Ordinary,[151] Title X, Book V of the Code makes one mention of a Superior in connection with the penal remedies. The text reads as follows: "Both the rebuke and warning may be given once or several times, depending upon the judgment and prudence of the Superior."[152]

Who then is this Superior? It is impossible from the wording of the text of canon 2309, § 6 to determine whether the word Superior refers to a religious Superior, or is a synonym for the Ordinary who is mentioned in another section of this same canon 2309 as well as in canons 2307 and 2308. From the context, however, it is apparent that the term Superior as it is used in canon 2309, § 6 is merely a synonym for the Ordinary and judge. As such, it does not extend the prerogative of imposing the penal remedies to anyone who is not mentioned in the other canons, but is rather a term which is intended to comprehend the Ordinary and the judge who were mentioned previously.

A study of the context seems to completely exclude the possibility that the term Superior refers to a third person. If the interpretation were otherwise, the canon would have to be taken to mean that the Ordinary is the author of the warning[153] and the rebuke,[154]

148 *Commentarium,* III, 492.

149 Cf. C. 1947; c. 2220, § 1; also Jone, *Commentarium,* III, 271; Coronata, *Institutiones,* III, 458, n. 1469.

150 Cf. c. 1950.

151 Cf. C. 1573, § 2.

152 C. 2309, § 6: Tam correptio quam monitio fieri potest semel vel pluries, pro Superioris arbitrio et prudentia.

153 C. 2307.

154 C. 2308-2309.

yet the decision of whether or not the warning or rebuke ought to be given once or several times is left to the judgement and prudence of a third person, the Superior. This, of course, is apparently not the mind of the legislator in this matter, because the remote contents of canons 2307-2308 together with canon 2309 exclude such an intervention of a heretofore unmentioned " Superior."

Authors such as O'Brien [155] and Quinn [156] are in accord with this position of the present writer that the context of the legislation on the use of the penal remedies points to the fact that the term " superior " of canon 2309, § 6 must be accepted as a synonym for those who are to impose a penal remedy upon a subject i. e., the Ordinary and judge.

4. COMPETENT ORDINARY OR JUDGE

It has been previously pointed out that the Roman Pontiff as an Ordinary may issue a penal remedy to any member of the Church anywhere in the world.[157] There is little need here to discuss the competency of the Pope in matters of discipline and correction. This competency is evident from the constitution of the Church.

The other Ordinaries, however, are limited in the extent of their competency to issue penal remedies. This limitation is set by law with reference to a certain territory or certain persons or both.

The residential Bishop is the ordinary and immediate shepherd over the territory of the diocese committed to his care,[158] and, once he has taken canonical possession of his diocese, he may exercise his authority over it in accord with the norms of the sacred canons. Likewise, those who occupy offices similar to a residential Bishop possess similar powers for their respective territories during their terms of office.[159] Thus the Vicars and Prefects Apostolic,[160] Abbots

[155] O'Brien, *The Provincial Religious Superior,* The Catholic University of America Canon Law Studies, n. 258 (Washington, D. C.: The Catholic University of America, Press, 1947), p. 246.

[156] H. G. Quinn, *The Particular Penal Precept,* The Catholic University of America Canon Law Studies n. 303 (Washington, D. C.: The Catholic University of America Press, 1953), p. 66.

[157] Cf. c. 198, § 1; c. 218.

[158] C. 334, § 1.

[159] Cf. *Supra,* Section F, p. 57.

[160] C. 294, § 1: . . . in suo territorio . . . .

and Prelates *nullius*,[161] Apostolic Administrators,[162] and, *sede vacante,* the Cathedral Chapter,[163] and the Vicar Capitular,[164] all may employ the penal remedies in their respective territories. These offices have reason for existence in so far as they are related to definite territories and the persons of those territories. The legislative, judicial and coactive power of a residential Bishop, and of those similar in the law of jurisdiction to a residential Bishop, is found to be radically united to their respective offices. These Ordinaries may use their power within the limits of the territory entrusted to their care, in every way in which the fulfillment of the duties of their offices may demand, provided that no limits have been placed on them by the higher constitutional authority of the Church.[165] In other words, these Ordinaries are competent to issue penal remedies within the limits of their proper territories as long as the Holy See has not withdrawn certain persons from the scope of the Ordinary's competency.

The Holy See has as a matter of law for most matters exempted certain religious living in a territory from the direct jurisdiction of the local Ordinary.[166] It has made different but somewhat similar provisions for travelers who are passing through his territory.[167] Neither of these groups are the proper subjects of these local Ordinaries; they are subject to their jurisdiction and correction only in those matters which are specified by law. Moreover, in the realm of judicial procedure, definite limitations have been placed on the competency of the local Ordinary and his *Officialis*.[168]

[161] C. 319, § 1: Praelati qui praesunt territorio proprio . . . ; c. 323, § 1: . . . easdem potestates ordinarias easdemque obligationes cum iisdem sanctionibus habet, quae competunt Episcopis residentialibus in propris diocesi.

[162] C. 312: Diocesis canonice erectae regimen . . . Administratori Apostolico vel in perpetuum vel ad tempus committit. Cf. cc. 314-315.

[163] C. 431, § 1: . . . ad Capitulum ecclesiae cathedralis regimen dioecesis devolvitur. . . .

[164] C. 432: . . . Vicarium Capitularem qui loco sui diocesim regat . . . ; c. 435, § 1: Sicut ad Capitulum ante deputationem Vicarii Capitularis, ita deinde ad Vicarium Capitularem transit ordinaria Episcopi jurisdictio. . . .

[165] Adapted from Roelker, *Precepts*, p. 42.

[166] Cf. c. 500.

[167] C. 14.

[168] Cf. c. 1557, where competence is reserved to the Holy See, therefore

Besides the exercise of jurisdiction in his territory, by reason of the superior-subject relationship which is established between the residential Bishop and his proper subjects in a territory, the Bishop may exercise non-judicial jurisdiction over them even when he or they are outside the boundary limits of the proper territory.[169] The relationship may thus be personal but based upon residence in a particular territory.

Since the judicial power of a residential Bishop is communicated to the diocesan judge by the bestowal of this latter office,[170] the competency of the *Officialis* is limited to the same extent as the judicial power of his Bishop. Judicial jurisdiction is territorial for the local Ordinary and may not be exercised outside the proper territory except for the rare cases envisioned by canons 401, § 1; 881, § 2 and 1637.[171]

Besides the jurisdictional relationship which is based upon residence in a territory, the competence of an Ordinary may be personal by reason of profession in an exempt clerical religious institute or a status acquired with such an institute. The Major Superior of such an institute is the Ordinary for his subjects[172] and accordingly has competency in their regard[173] no matter where they might be, unless he was lost it by some provision of law.

Over and above the competency which exists between the Ordinary and his proper subjects by reason either of a territorial or personal bond, the provisions of penal law also recognize instances when the residential Bishop is competent to correct and punish even those who are not his proper subjects. Except for those cases whose consideration is reserved to the Roman Pontiff or the Holy See,[174] the local Ordinary has competence over all cases involving delicts which have been committed in his territory.[175]

the local tribunals are absolutely incompetent in these matters and in regard to these persons; c. 1560-1568, relative competence and incompetence of local tribunals for various reasons.

169 C. 201, § 3.

170 Cf. Roelker, *Precepts*, p. 125.

171 Cf. c. 201, § 2.

172 C. 198, § 1: . . . pro suis vero subditis. . . .

173 C. 501.

174 C. 1557.

175 C. 1566: Ratione delicti reus forum sortitur in loco patrati delicti.

On this basis, the local Ordinary or judge has competence over subjects and non-subjects alike whenever a delict has been committed by them in his territory. The Code also provides that even though the person leaves the scene of the crime and departs from the particular territory, the judge of the place where the crime was committed has the right to cite the delinquent to trial and pass sentence on him.[176]

In the realm of delicts, normally the correction of an exempt religious is a matter which is handled by the Holy See and by those Superiors who are recognized as competent to do so by the constitutions of the particular institute.[177] If, however, an exempt religious commits a delict while being lawfully outside his religious house and remains unpunished by his proper Superior, even though the latter was duly informed of the matter, then the local Ordinary is competent to punish him.[178]

To conclude this section, therefore, it may be stated that the competence of the Ordinary or judge to impose penal remedies is determined by the relationship between the Ordinary and his proper subjects established by reason of territorial and/or personal bonds; and between the Ordinary and non-subjects by reason of a territorial bond resulting from some particular specification of law.

Section G. Subjects of Penal Remedies

This section is the converse of the previous section and considers the question: "Who are the persons who may be given a penal remedy by a competent Ordinary or Judge?"

1. The Clergy and Laity

The pre-Code Instruction of the Sacred Congregation for Bishops and Regulars (1880) specified the clergy as subjects for the application of the canonical remedies.[179] No mention was made of the laity. It may be recalled that at the time of the

176 C. 1566, § 2.

177 Cf. C. 501.

178 C. 616.—N. B. Unlawful sojurn outside the religious house bars the privilege of exemption, and makes a delinquent religious the subject of punishment from the local Bishop.

179 Cf. *Sacra Haec*, n. 1: . . . disciplinam correctionemque clericorum. . . .

issuance of this Instruction, it was the clear intention of the Holy See to counteract the effects of conditions in the world which were almost everywhere impeding the Church from applying its external action to ecclesiastical matters and persons.[180] In order to protect its right and position, there was apparently a concerted effort made to effectively keep at least the canonical discipline of the clergy within the competence of ecclesiastical control. Thus, *Sacra Haec* with its revisions and adaptations of the Church's system of discipline and procedure was issued specifically for the clergy.

In the same manner The Instruction of the Sacred Congregation for the Propagation of the Faith (1883)[181] and the Third Plenary Council of Baltimore (1884)[182] made provisions for the use of the canonical remedies in regard to the clergy. In these provisions there were no indications that these canonical measures as such were to be employed also in respect to the laity.

While it may be that no thought was given to the possibility of including the laity within the scope of the above legislation, it is more than likely that the matter was given serious consideration and was thought to be ill-advised for the conditions of that time. Messmer is inclined to this view. In presenting a preliminary plan for his commentary on *Sacra Haec* he remarks, "We exclude, therefore, from our treatise the criminal procedure against laymen. Against these the Church nowadays proceeds only in the case of very great necessity, viz., when by their conduct they give great public scandal." [183] Similarly, in his commentary on *Cum Magnopere,* Smith makes it clear that, "The Instruction applies only to ecclesiastics, not to laics. In fact, at the present day, the Church, also with us [in the United States], finds it almost impossible to proceed judicially against laics, even when they commit offences strictly ecclesiastical." [184]

Although much of the bigotry and lack of toleration toward the

[180] Cf. *Sacra Haec,* Introduction.

[181] *Cum Magnopere,* n. I: . . . disciplinam correptionemque clericorum . . . .

[182] Conc. Plen. Balt. III., nn. 308-310—*Acta et Decreta,* pp. 176-178: . . . in causis criminalibus clericorum. . . .

[183] *Canonical Procedure,* p. 26.

[184] *New Procedure,* p. 19; contents of brackets inserted by present writer.

discipline of the Church, which was associated with the nineteenth century, has subsided in the present day, the current conditions cannot be said to be greatly different in regard to the Church's use of judicial procedure against the laity. Present conditions do seem, however, to be suitable for the effective extra-judicial use of the penal remedies upon the laity when the cases would warrant it. An official warning or precept from the local Ordinary, given either directly or through his personal representative, would seem to be a very powerful preventive measure against possible scandal and laxity of the faithful toward errors in the spheres of faith or morals. Indeed such disciplinary action may be just the means needed to call attention to the seriousness of a situation and recall the person from possible crime and excommunication.

To consider whether or not the use of the penal remedies in the discipline of the laity is advisable seems, however, to be only of speculative interest. A comparison of the pre-Code legislation and the provisions of the Code of Canon Law on the matter reveals that the Code does not follow the previous legislation. The specifications of *Sacra Haec* and *Cum Magnopere* for the use of the canonical remedies upon the clergy have been deleted by the Code. Since no such specification is made, it seems reasonable to conclude that no such specification may be presumed. The Code merely points out various cases when the remedies are to be used, making no provision that these disciplinary measures are for clerics, or that the laity are not included whenever they are involved in these cases. It seems therefore that the prescriptions of the Code must be accepted as being of general import and concern not only clerics, but the laity as well. Among the authors who agree with this position, one may refer to Coronata [185] and Ayrinhac-Lydon.[186]

Who then are the members of the clergy and laity of the Church who may be subject to receive a penal remedy? It would seem that all of the faithful who are subject to correction by a competent Ordinary or Judge and are morally capable of committing a delict would qualify for possible inclusion within this category.

185 *Institutiones*, IV, 282, n. 1838.

186 *Penal Legislation*, p. 136, n. 179.

2. MORAL CAPACITY TO COMMIT AN ECCLESIASTICAL DELICT

The moral capacity of a person to commit an ecclesiastical delict depends upon the following factors: 1) the reception of Baptism; 2) the possession of the use of reason; 3) sufficient age; 4) the presence of enough facts and circumstances to indicate sufficient *dolus* or *culpa* to constitute responsibility.

1. The fundamental requisite for such capacity is that a person must be a member of the Church. This, of course, is effected by Baptism.[187] Only through the reception of the Sacrament of Baptism does a human being acquire the juridic status of *person* in the Church of Christ and a member of the society of the Church.[188]

2. Besides being baptized, the person must also have achieved the use of reason,[189] for delinquency results from responsible human acts. Unless there is proof to the contrary, this is presumed once the child has completed his seventh year.[190]

3. The third requisite for moral capacity to commit an ecclesiastical delict is sufficient maturity of age to do so. This stage is not easy to determine. The Code states that minors who have not attained the age of puberty are excused from all *latae sententiae* penalties and should be punished with educational correction rather than with censures and severe vindictive penalties.[191] The law does not imply that these minors who have not attained the age of puberty are free from all responsibility for their actions or that they are incapable of committing ecclesiastical delicts. Indeed, as soon as they enjoy the use of reason, minors' acts are imputable to them in varying degrees, and may justly be punished.[192]

Canon 2200, § 2 states that when there is an external violation of a law, it is presumed in the external forum that the person acted

187 C. 87.

188 Cf. Cicognani, *Canon Law* (2. ed., Westminster, Md.: The Newman Bookshop, 1934), p. 562.

189 C. 12.

190 C. 88.

191 Cf. C. 2230; Cicognani, *Canon Law*, p. 564; Ayrinhac-Lydon, *Penal Legislation*, p. 43.

192 Ayrinhac-Lydon, *Penal Legislation*, p. 43.

with a deliberate will of violating the law, until the contrary is proven.[193] Whenever a material delict has been committed in the external forum, therefore, there is a legal presumption that the person who committed it acted with *dolus* and responsibility. This presumption admits of proof to the contrary, by arguments based on either a lack of sufficient knowledge or a lack of freedom of will.[194] Once there has been an external violation of law, however, a presumption of guilt is established, and the person's innocence or lack of culpability is not presumed, but must be proven.

Since no distinction is made in canon 2200, § 2 between adults or minors, *impuberes* or *puberes,* the law must be understood to apply to all who are bound by the laws of the Church. When there has been a transgression of a penal law in the external forum, the transgressor is presumed to have acted with *dolus. Impuberes* are not exempted from this presumption. Until the transgressor has exonerated himself, he is subject to punishment according to the nature and gravity of the case.

When cases involve *impuberes,* however, a great diminution of culpability will most often be present due to lack of knowledge, advertence and consent resulting from immaturity of age and its accompanying ignorance.[195] The law provides that minor age usually lessens imputability and that this lessening increases in direct proportion as the age of the individual is closer to infancy.[196] For these reasons the Code, while not excusing their misconduct, states that other punishments, which could be educational and contribute to their training, should be used upon *impuberes,* rather than *ipso facto* penalties, censures and severe vindictive penalties.[197]

Whenever an *impuber* is subject to the educational punishments prescribed by the Code, it is the opinion of the present writer that the penal remedies may be employed. Indeed it seems that these remedies could be very efficacious provided they are adapted to the age of the child and the circumstances of the case; and may serve

193 C. 2200, § 2: Posita externa legis violatione, dolus in foro externo praesumitur, donec contrarium probetur.

194 Cf. c. 2200, § 1.

195 C. 2202; c. 2218.

196 C. 2204.

197 Cf. c. 2230; Ayrinhac-Lydon, *Penal Legislation,* p. 43.

well both in crime-prevention and crime-repression among the *impuberes.*

An even greater scope for the penal remedies may be realized in regard to minors who have advanced beyond the age of puberty. While still lacking the maturity of adults, these nevertheless are seen to have greater responsibility for their delinquency, and their responsibility heightens to fullness as they advance to the age of twenty-one years.[198]

Whether by single-handed effort or by activity in groups or gangs, youths are capable of widespread scandal, destruction, violence, various serious disturbances of public order and ecclesiastical delinquency. For these offenses the provisions of canons 2307-2311 cannot be overlooked in regard to their application to minors. The timely use of the warning, rebuke or precept, from the Ordinary to the individual offenders in these cases may best serve as preservative measures from crime, and, at the same time, be the means of assisting these youths to live useful and fruitful lives as adults. A mild form of surveillance, whereby the delinquent is obliged periodically to report on his conduct to his pastor or lay custodian, may also be used when there is a grave case and danger of a youth lapsing again into crime.

4. Besides the factor of age, the person must also be morally capable of sufficient *culpa* or *dolus*[199] to qualify as someone who could a) commit a delict, b) be in the proximate occasion of commiting a delict, c) be the cause of scandal, d) be responsible for a grave disturbance of order, or e) be in danger of relapsing into crime—for these are the occasions required for the use of the penal remedies.[200] The person must therefore be mentally, physically and emotionally capable of responsible human activity. These personal characteristics are presumed whenever there is an external violation of law, unless the contrary is proven.[201] The lack of such moral capacity may be proven only when either habitual insanity or drunkenness, inculpable ignorance, physical force, fear and

198 *Ad mentem* c. 2204.

199 Cf. cc. 2199-2209.

200 Cf. cc. 2306-2311; c. 1933, § 4.

201 C. 2200, § 2.

passion are present to the extent that culpability for human action is abolished beyond the pale of serious sin.[202]

3. SUBJECT AND COMPETENT ORDINARY

Besides the moral capacity to commit a delict, for the issuance of a penal remedy there must also exist a juridic relationship between the person being corrected and the Ordinary who is imposing the punishment. As was seen in the preceding section 5, this bond may be established in several ways: a) by reason of a relationship which arises on the basis of territorial jurisdiction; and b) by a personal relationship.

a. *Relationship Derived From Territorial Jurisdiction*

(1) Domicile and Quasi-Domicile

The most common basis for ecclesiastical discipline is the juridic relationship which is established between an Ordinary and his proper subject by reason of the latter's domicile or quasi-domicile within the territory of the Ordinary.[203] This relationship has foundation in the constitution of the Church whereby the residential Bishop, by reason of his office, is the immediate shepherd of the diocese committed to his care.[204] As a result of his canonical mission from the Roman Pontiff and canonical possession of his diocese, the residential Bishop receives the exercise of jurisdiction over his particular territory.[205] He thus has the right and duty of governing his diocese in spiritual and temporal matters by employing his legislative, judicial and coactive powers in accord with the legal framework established by the Code of Canon Law.[206] The residential Bishop is thereby obliged to enforce the observance of the laws of the Church,[207] and he must be vigilant lest abuses creep in upon ecclesiastical discipline. He must also be careful that the purity of faith and morals of both the clergy and laity is safeguarded.[208]

202 Cf. c. 2201; c. 2202; c. 2205; c. 2206; 2218, § 2.

203 C. 94, § 1.

204 C. 334, § 1.

205 Cc. 109; 332; 334, § 2.

206 C. 335, § 1.

207 C. 336, § 1.

208 Cf. C. 336, § 2.

Canon 335 provides that the Bishop is to exercise his authority in accordance with the norms of the sacred canons.[209] From this provision it is clearly specified that a definite plan for the exercise of his power is established for the Bishop by the Code. Hence the matter is left neither in the realm of uncertainty nor to arbitrary choice. A segment of this general plan states that the power of jurisdiction may be exercised directly only upon one's own subjects.[210] Since the possession of a domicile or quasi-domicile in a certain territory makes their possessors the proper subjects of the Ordinary of that territory,[211] it also makes them the subjects of his direct exercise of the power of jurisdiction.

In the exercise of his non-judicial jurisdiction over his subjects, the Ordinary may act when he is outside his proper territory; and also when his subjects are within or outside the limits of the Ordinary's territory unless the nature of the case or the law specifies to the contrary.[212]

On the other hand, when the Ordinary or the *Officialis* exercises judicial jurisdiction, this must be done within the limits of the proper territory unless the rare exceptions provided for by canons 401, § 1, 881, § 2, and 1637 are present.[213] As long as they are in their own territory, the Ordinary or his *Officialis* is competent to proceed judicially against those who are their proper subjects by reason of domicile or quasi-domicile, even though they may be outside the Ordinary's territory at that time.[214]

When punishments are inflicted by the use of judicial jurisdiction, the Judge is further limited to matters which are public delicts,[215] the penal sanctions provided for by canons 2168-2194 being withdrawn from his jurisdiction.[216] The term public is here understood as used in the sense of canon 2197, i. e. in respect to a delict which is already known to the people of a community, or else

[209] C. 335, § 1: . . . ad normam sacrorum canonum exercenda. . . .

[210] C. 201, § 1.

[211] C. 94, § 1.

[212] Cf. C. 201, § 3.

[213] C. 201, § 2.

[214] C. 1561, §§ 1, 2.

[215] C. 1933, § 1.

[216] C. 1933, § 2.

is either of such a nature or accompanied by such circumstances, that its publicity can and must prudently be judged as readily to ensue.[217] There no such restriction on the exercise of non-judicial jurisdiction.

The residential Ordinary may judicially and extra-judicially employ the penal remedies upon those persons who are his subjects by reason of domicile and quasi-domicile within the provisions of law. Thus, when his subjects are present within his territory, the Ordinary may impose penal remedies upon them for matters which involve delicts of the: 1) general law of the Church; [218] or 2) precepts; [219] and 3) particular territorial laws.[220] When absent from the territory but with the intention of returning, these persons are subject to the penal remedies lawfully inflicted by the Ordinary of their domicile or quasi-domicile whenever there is a delict involving: 1) the general law of the Church,[221] unless this does not oblige in the place where they are traveling [222] (an eventuality which is not very probable); 2) personal laws; [223] 3) precepts; [224] and 4) particular territorial laws of his own territory when their transgression would inflict injury in his territory.[225] The person would not be subject, however, to correction by his Ordinary in respect to the particular laws of his domicile or quasi-domicile which would not inflict harm upon his proper territory.[226]

It may be noted here that, as far as the relationship needed in order to be subject to the correction of the local Ordinary is concerned, there is no practical difference between the persons having a domicile or quasi-domicile in the Ordinary's territory.[227] Both

217 C. 2197: Publicum, si iam divulgatum est aut talibus contigit seu versatur in adiunctis ut prudenter iudicari possit et debeat facile divulgatum iri.

218 C. 13, § 1.

219 C. 24.

220 C. 13, § 2.

221 C. 201, § 3.

222 C. 14, § 1, 3°.

223 C. 14, § 1, 1°.

224 C. 24.

225 C. 14, § 1, 1°.

226 C. 14, § 1, 1°.

227 Cf. Cicognani, *Canon Law*, p. 574.

types of residence create a juridic bond. Each status establishes the Ordinary of the territory as their Ordinary,[228] and makes them subject to that Ordinary's correction both judicially[229] and extra-judicially.[230] The penal remedies would, of course, be included as one of the methods of correction which could be employed by the Ordinary.

There is nothing essential to the nature of the domicile and quasi-domicile which would militate against a possession of several of them by the same person. It is clearly possible for a person to have at least two voluntary domiciles; a cumulation of domicile and quasi-domiciles, or several quasi-domiciles at the same time.[231] No matter how multiplied the relationship of Ordinary-to-subject may become by reason of the number of domiciles and quasi-domiciles, the exercise of jurisdiction by each Ordinary is not hindered as long as the provisions of the law are observed.[232] A person is subject to correction from the Ordinary of each territory in which he has a domicile or quasi-domicile.

The collective possession of domiciles and quasi-domiciles does not continually keep accumulating, however. Except for the necessary domiciles of canon 93, § 1[233] domiciles and quasi-domiciles can be lost by the presence of two elements: 1) physical departure from the territory, together with 2) the intention of not returning and of not resuming residence there.[234] The necessary domiciles of canon 93, § 1 can be lost only by the cessation of the bond of subjection upon which they are based.[235] When a person loses a domicile or quasi-domicile, the basis for correction by that local Ordinary ceases, unless it continues by reason of some other title, such as that of canon 1566, § 1 (*in loco patrati delicti*) or of canon 14, § 1, 2° (travelers) and canon 14, § 2 (vagrants).

228 C. 94, § 1.

229 C. 201, §§ 1, 2; c. 1561.

230 C. 201, § 1, § 3.

231 Cf. Coronata, *Institutiones*, I, 143, n. 127.

232 Cf. Roelker, *Precepts*, p. 60.

233 I. e. A wife who is not legitimately separated from her husband or a minor who is still under the care of parents or guardian.

234 C. 95.

235 Cf. Beste, *Introductio*, p. 145.

(2) Persons Without Domicile or Quasi-Domicile

In addition to the relation which exists between the Ordinary and those who are his proper subjects by reason of domicile or quasi-domicile, the law also provides for the establishment of other juridic bonds between the local Ordinary and persons who are within the limits of his ecclesiastical territory. Even though they may not be his proper subjects, the Ordinary nevertheless has some jurisdiction over non-subjects while they are physically present within his territory. In this manner the law also makes provision for the proper supervision and protection of the faith, morals and ecclesiastical discipline against any possible evils caused by travelers or vagrants. This exercise of authority is for the benefit of the whole society of the Church, the welfare of the Church in that particular community, and for the spiritual well-being of the individuals who may be involved.

Vagrants (*Vagi*)

Vagrants are those members of the Church who have neither domicile nor quasi-domicile anywhere.[236] In order that their status will not be without government by ecclesiastical authority, and not be the occasion of spiritual harm either to the other members of the Church or to themselves, the law specifies that vagrants have as their proper Ordinary, the Ordinary of any territory in which they happen to be.[237] As long as they are physically present in any territory, therefore, all vagrants are subject to the local Ordinary in the same manner and to the same extent as if they had a domicile or quasi-domicile there. This subjection is equally applicable *in favorabilibus* and *in odiosis.*[238] By this legally established juridic bond between the local Ordinary and the vagrant, the latter is directly accountable to the former for the observance of both the general laws of the Church and the particular laws of the territory.[239] The vagrant is thus subject to punishment by the local Ordinary for all delicts committed against these laws.[240] In

236 C. 91.

237 C. 94, § 2.

238 Cf. Coronata, *Institutiones*, I, 136, n. 122.

239 C. 14, § 2.

240 Cf. Cappello, *De Censuris*, p. 19, n. 19.

judicial matters, the vagrant has the forum of the place where he is as his proper forum.[241]

This relationship between the vagrant and the local Ordinary has the twofold characteristic of being both territorial and temporary. It is territorial because its existence is completely dependent upon the vagrant's presence within the confines of the local Ordinary's territory; and temporary by reason of the transitory nature of the vagrant's stay there. Since the vagrant has neither the intention nor the actual length of stay which is required to establish a domicile or quasi-domicile, no abiding bond of residence in the locality can be claimed. Once the vagrant has left the territory, his juridic relationship with the Ordinary completely ceases (unless a jurisdictional bond has been established by the commission of a delict),[242] and begins anew in relation to another local Ordinary.

Travelers (*Peregrini*)

The traveler is a person who has a domicile or quasi-domicile and, although at the present time he is out of his proper territory, he has the intention of returning to it as his place of residence.[243] By his intention to return, the traveler retains his proper territory, and the Ordinary of that territory remains his proper Ordinary.[244]

Because the traveler is still subject to his own proper Ordinary in many matters, the law specifies a more limited relationship between the traveler and the local Ordinary than exists between the vagrant and the local Ordinary. In the realm of crime-prevention and punishments, however, the local Ordinary may exercise quite extensive coactive jurisdiction over the conduct of the traveler journeying in his territory. As Coronata notes, the Ordinary's jurisdiction not only extends directly to his proper subjects, but also often extends indirectly to non-subjects for one reason or another based on a provision of law.[245]

As custodian of the common good and protector of the social

[241] C. 1563.

[242] Cf. c. 1566.

[243] Cf. c. 91.

[244] C. 95; c. 94.

[245] Cf. *Institutiones*, I, 329, n. 282.

order of the Church, the local Ordinary enjoys the exercise of coactive power in his diocese. He is bound to urge the observance of the laws of the Church,[246] and must be vigilant against any abuse or danger to the purity of faith and morals among the clergy and people.[247] Conversely, the traveler is obliged to obey all the general laws of the Church except those which are not in force in the territory through which he is traveling.[248] Since there would hardly be a local dispensation from the general penal law of the Church, it is reasonable to state here that the traveler is subject to such laws wherever he might go. The traveler is responsible to the local Ordinary for infractions against the general penal law of the Church, and he is subject to the punishments specified by the Code for such infractions. As custodian of the common good, the local Ordinary may impose the penal remedies upon travelers as well as upon his own subjects for any misconduct which involves the commission of delicts or the specific cases included in canons 2307-2311.

Furthermore, the local Ordinary is the guardian of the public order in his territory. He may impose particular laws, even penal laws, upon all who may be in his territory, in order to fulfill this duty of his office. The traveler, by provision of law, is subject to such particular legislation.[249]

The concept of what constitutes a disturbance of the public order as referred to by canon 14 is not given in the Code, and is not uniformly explained by those who write on the subject. A very fine synthesis of numerous opinions has been presented by Esswein.[250] He states that it is the general consensus of opinion that those laws concern public order which tend to avoid a common danger and harm to the inhabitants.

246 C. 336, § 1.

247 C. 336, § 2.

248 C. 14, § 1, 3°.

249 Cf. c. 14, § 1, 2°.

250 Esswein, *The Extrajudicial Coercive Powers of Ecclesiastical Superiors*, The Catholic University of America Canon Law Studies, n. 127 (Washington, D.C.: The Catholic University of America Press, 1941), p. 80-81. He bases his statement upon a consideration of the views of Augustine, Blatt, Cappello, Chelodi, Claeys Bouuaert-Simenon, Coronata, DeMeester, Michiels, Noldin-Schmitt, Sole, Van Hove, Vermeersch-Creusen, Wernz, Wernz-Vidal, *et al.*

In regard to the public order, Cappello agrees with the position of Vermeersch-Creusen that this concept is not embraced in the objective of all particular penal legislation, but is only in those laws (even non-penal laws) which are concerned with averting a common danger or common loss. He believes that travelers are not essentiallly obliged to contribute positively to the common good of another territory, but that they are obliged to refrain from inflicting injury to the common welfare there.[251]

More specifically, it seems that the laws which are for the public order include those which concern: the external good order in public gatherings or processions, etc.; public peace and tranquility; the external and public aspects in the life and conduct of the clergy; anything which concerns the elimination of some common harm or public scandal; proper respect for the exercise of ecclesiastical jurisdiction; laws of commerce; the transportation of weapons; the exercise of public power and public office.[252] Any particular legislation which involves these and similar disturbances of public order command the obedience of travelers as well as the inhabitants of a locality, and disobedience makes the offender subject to the correction of the local Ordinary. Such correction could, of course, include the wise use of the penal remedies in the various aspects of crime prevention and repression as employed by the Code.

(3) Members of Religious Institutes

The members of religious institutes in the Church form a notable segment of those persons who are present in the territory of the local Ordinary. By the fact that they are assigned to a religious house within his territory, religious become subject to the legislation and correction of the local Ordinary, within the limitations established by law and privilege.[253] The relationship which results from this fact is subject to qualifications which must be considered at this time.

[251] Cappello, *De Censuris*, p. 20.

[252] Cf. Cappello, *De Censuris*, p. 20; Coronata, *Institutiones*, I, 29, n. 15; Regatillo, *Institutiones*, I, 69, n. 72.

[253] Cf. cc. 500; 615; 616; 618, § 1; 1563; 965; 956; 1221, § 1; 1216; 1566; 1561.

The local Ordinary, by reason of the constitution of the Church, exercises the jurisdiction which is attached to his office over all of his territory. In the exercise of his jurisdiction, Roelker notes that the Ordinary may use his power in every way in which the duties of his office may demand, provided that no limitation has been placed by higher constitutional authority of the Church.[254]

The relationship existing between the local Ordinary and the religious who are assigned to his territory has definite limitations set by the Roman Pontiff as supreme legislation. These limitations of the Ordinary's exercise of jurisdiction over religious have been in the form of enactments of law and privileges of exemption[255] granted to the religious institute by the Holy See. As a result of these limitations, the extent of the Ordinary's exercise of jurisdiction is in direct inverse proportion of the exemptions which have been granted to these religious.

Since religious are members of the Church and also members of a particular society within the Church, they are subject to two kinds of obligations: 1) those which the Church imposes upon clerics and laity; and 2) those which result from the rule and constitution of their institute. Besides being subject to the Roman Pontiff (as members of the Church and of their society and by reason of their vow of obedience), religious are also subject to two sources of authority within the limitation of the legislation of the Church and the provisions of the rule and constitution of their institute: the local Ordinary and their religious superiors. By the privilege of exemption, the local Ordinary's exercise of jurisdiction over some religious is limited by the Roman Pontiff to himself and exercised either personally or by someone designated by the supreme legislator.

[254] Cf. *Precepts*, p. 12.

[255] The privilege of exemption implies two things: withdrawal from the jurisdictional power of one superior; and subjection to some other authority. In regard to religious, it seems that certain religious organizations are withdrawn from the jurisdiction of the local Ordinary and placed under the immediate authority of the Roman Pontiff alone. The latter, in turn, ordinarily governs them by means of superiors who are members of their respective society. The law expressly states what power the local Ordinaries have over these religious.—Cf. O'Brien, *The Exemption of Religious in Church Law* (Milwaukee: Bruce, 1943), p. 3.

Religious are subject to the local Ordinary in varying degrees:

1. Regulars, both men and women who take solemn vows (except those nuns who are not subject to superiors of Regulars) together with their houses and churches are exempt from the local Ordinary except for those cases which are expressly provided for by law.[256] For Regulars, then, exemption is the rule and exceptions to this rule have to be proven.[257] This exemption applies to professed religious and also to novices.[258] Creusen-Ellis note, however, that exemption does not extend to postulants, nor to lay subjects of the local Ordinary who happen to be in the monastery of an exempt institute.[259]

Noteworthy exceptions to the exemption enjoyed by these Regulars principally concern the erection of houses,[260] the exercise of public worship and divine services [261] and especially the administration of the sacrament of penance.[262] For nuns the limitation on their exemption also extends to the proper observance of the papal cloister [263] and the management of certain temporal goods.[264] Those nuns who pronounce only simple vows ordinarily do not enjoy such exemption, nor do those who are not under the jurisdiction of a Regular superior,[265] and they are therefore dependent upon the local Ordinary who acts as a representative of the Holy See.

2. Institutes with simple vows do not enjoy the privilege of exemption unless it has been especially conceded to them,[266] and general exemption is rarely granted to these congregations. This privilege has, however, been accorded to the Redemptorists, Passionists and, by a special form, to the Daughters of Charity of

[256] C. 615.

[257] Bouscaren-Ellis, *Canon Law*, p. 292.

[258] Cf. c. 615.

[259] Cf. *Religious Men And Women In The Code*, p. 223.

[260] Cc. 497; 1162.

[261] Cc. 612; 1261; 336.

[262] C. 874.

[263] C. 603, § 1.

[264] C. 533, § 1, 1°.

[265] Cf. Creusen-Ellis, *Religious Men and Women in the Code*, p. 223.

[266] C. 618, § 1.

St. Vincent de Paul. These are subject to the jurisdiction of the local Ordinary only in the same matters as Regulars or according to the terms of their decree of exemption. In regard to all other congregations of pontifical right (i. e., those who have at least received the *decretum laudis* from the Apostolic See), the power of the local Ordinary is limited, though by no means in the same manner as in the case of the exempt religious.[267] Some of these restrictions on the jurisdiction of the local Ordinary are listed in canon 618, § 2.[268]

3. The local Ordinary has full authority over religious of diocesan right, within the limits of the Code and the provisions of their constitution.[269]

The Code provides that in all matters in which religious are subject to the local Ordinary, he may coerce them with penalties.[270] This principle for the use of coercive power also includes, of course, the appropriate use of the penal remedies.[271]

Besides the existence of a religious house within the limits of his territory, there may be several other bases for a juridic bond between the local Ordinary and persons who are assigned to such a house. A postulant or novice who is a minor, retains the necessary domicile of his parent or guardian, and may also acquire a quasi-domicile in the site of the postulancy or novitiate.[272] If the postulant or novice is an adult and in the territory where he will remain permanently (e. g., a *sui iuris* monastery) he may acquire a voluntary domicile during the time of the postulancy or novitiate,

267 Schaefer, *De Religiosis* (4. ed., Roma: Typis Polyglottis Vaticanis, 1947), p. 171.

268 For an extensive list of the provisions of law concerning the relation of the local Ordinary to religious, cf. Schaefer, *De Religiosis*, pp. 172-180; O'Brien, *The Exemption of Religious In Church Law*, pp. 283-286; Bouscaren-Ellis, *Canon Law*, pp. 292-294.

269 Cf. c. 492, § 2; Schaefer, *De Religiosis*, p. 171.

270 C. 619.

271 It may be noted here that the special privilege of exemption from censures of the local Ordinary enjoyed by the Mendicants and the Jesuits does not extend to vindictive penalties or to the penal remedies.—cf. Esswein, *The Extrajudicial Coercive Powers of Ecclesiastical Superiors*, p. 93; O'Brien, *The Exemption Of Religious In Church Law*, p. 49.

272 Cf. Sipos, *Enchiridion*, p. 71; Beste, *Introductio*, p. 144.

which after profession becomes a necessary domicile.[273] On the other hand, if he is to enjoy no such stability of assignment at that particular place after the completion of his novitiate, he acquires a quasi-domicile there.

In general these persons are subject to correction by the local Ordinary by reason of their domicile or quasi-domicile. An exception to this general rule, however, exists in the case of a novice of Regulars. By law he enjoys all the privileges of exemption which have been granted to his Order.[274]

Regatillo presents another possibility of a religious as being subject to a local Ordinary on a basis other than the location of the religious house. He considers the case of a religious who is temporarily residing out of the cloister or religious house by indult of the Apostolic See or local Ordinary.[275] Although exclaustrated, this person remains bound by his vows in so far as their observance is compatible with his present situation. He likewise shares in the spiritual privileges of his community. By reason of his vow of obedience, this exclaustrated religious is legally subject to the Ordinary of the place where he happens to reside, instead of his proper religious superior.[276] It is conceivable therefore that by freely choosing the place of residence during his period of exclaustration, the religious could establish a voluntary quasi-domicile in the territory of some local Ordinary and thereby be subject to his correction.

Religious who are not the proper subjects of a local Ordinary are still subject to his correction *ratione delicti patrati.* This authority would, of course, be subject to modification in conformity with the constitutions of the religious institute and the provisions of the Code. In these matters, as in others, the least power of the Ordinary would exist in relation to Regulars. The Code states that if a Regular commits a delict outside the limits of his religious house and is not properly punished by his superior even after the latter has been informed of the matter, then the local Ordinary may punish the delinquent.[277] In case a Regular illegitimately

[273] Sipos, *Enchiridion,* p. 71.

[274] C. 615.

[275] Regatillo, *Institutiones,* I, 148.

[276] C. 639.

[277] C. 616, § 2.

travels outside his house, he loses his exemption,[278] and is subject to the local Ordinary's authority and correction in the same manner as any other non-exempt religious.

All non-exempt religious are subject to the local Ordinary's correction based at least upon the indirect exercise of his jurisdiction *ratione delicti patrati.* Such correction would include the use of the penal remedies. Nor would the local Ordinary be obliged to wait until a crime has certainly been committed before he may act. As custodian of the common good, the local Ordinary may also employ the preventive and repressive remedies whenever the conditions comprehended by the Code in canons 2307-2311 are present, i. e., whenever a religious who is subject to the correction of the Ordinary is judged to be in the proximate occasion of committing a delict, or upon whom an inquiry has left a grave suspicion that he has committed a delict; whenever the religious' conduct has given rise to scandal or a grave disturbance of order; whenever the gravity of the case warrants it, and especially if it concerns a religious who is in danger of relapsing into the same crime which he has previously committed.

b. *Relationship Resulting from a Personal Bond*

A juridic bond may also be established with an Ordinary on a basis other than a person's association with his territory. This type of bond is personal, and affects subjects regardless of their dwelling-place,[279] or even though they may be outside their religious house and beyond the limits of their province.[280] Such a bond exists between the members of an exempt clerical religious institute and their Major Superiors. These Superiors, it must be recalled, are included in the classification of Ordinaries in regard to their subjects,[281] and by concession of the Roman Pontiff, they possess the exercise of jurisdiction.[282]

This type of juridic relationship results from the person's pro-

[278] C. 616, § 1.

[279] Cf. O'Brien, *The Exemption of Religious in Church Law*, p. 30.

[280] Schaefer, *De Religiosis*, p. 196.

[281] C. 198, § 1: . . . pro suis vero subditis Superiores maiores in religionibus clericalibus exemptis.

[282] Cf. Roelker, *Precepts*, p. 43.

fession in an exempt clerical institute.[283] By reason of religious profession and the pronouncement of the public vows of religion which accompany his profession,[284] the religious makes himself subject to his Superiors, and obliges himself to obey them in accord with the provisions of the Code [285] and the rule and constitution of the Institute.[286]

Since his Major Superiors are Ordinaries, this professed religious of an exempt clerical institute is subject to receive penal remedies or other ecclesiastical punishments from these Superiors if the occasion would ever be present for their use.[287]

Besides the personal juridic bond which is produced by religious profession and public vows in an exempt clerical institute, a similar

283 Cf. Coronata, *Institutiones*, I, 329, n. 282.

284 Cc. 574; 487; cf. Schaefer, *De Religiosis*, p. 538, n. 940.

285 Cc. 489; 593.

286 C. 578, 2°; 501.

287 Schaefer notes that Major Superiors in exempt clerical institutes may impose canonical punishments of canon 2216, including the penal remedies. —*De Religiosis*, p. 203. He also states, however, that while *per se* the use of the penal remedies requires jurisdiction in the external forum; nevertheless, they may also be inflicted by the use of public dominative power, because this power is employed by every lesser society to govern its members.—*Op. cit.*, p. 204. While Beste lists the issuing of penal remedies as one of the facets of the power of jurisdiction, he allows that they may be also given by someone having dominative power.—*Introductio*, pp. 351; 350. Regatillo also claims that those persons who possess dominative power may issue the penal remedies.—*Institutiones*, I, 440, n. 655.

When compared to the provisions of the Code, these opinions produce some confusion. There is, of course, no contradiction in the idea that the scope of dominative power may include such measures as a warning, rebuke, precept, or surveillance, for the proper governing of the members of a society. However, the Code requires that the penal remedies be issued by those who are Ordinaries or Judges.—Cf. cc. 2307-2311. It may also be pointed out that, although the Code prescribes the use of warnings prior to the dismissal of religious, the only mention of the penal remedies in reference to these warnings is made relative to the dismissal of exempt clerical religious.—Cf. c. 661, § 1. The Superiors of these latter have jurisdiction; the Major Superiors are Ordinaries.—Cf. cc. 501 and 198.

For the religious Superiors who are Ordinaries, there is, of course, no difficulty. These may certainly employ the penal remedies of the Code.—Cf. cc. 2307-2311. For all Superiors who are not Ordinaries, however, it seems that dominative power, of itself, would not be sufficient basis for relationship may result between the religious Ordinary and a candidate who acquires a status in the institute by reason of an implied promise or agreement. Such a status is acquired by novices and postulants when they freely place themselves under the authority of the Superiors of the institute which they wish to join. Upon their entry, they assume at least an implicit obligation to obey their Superiors [288] as long as they retain their status in the institute.

Acceptance to the postulancy begins at the moment the candidate freely, and with the consent of the Superior, begins to dwell in the religious house as an aspirant to the institute.[289] Once the postulant is thus accepted, he becomes a subject of the jurisdiction of the religious Ordinary.[290]

The novitiate begins with the reception of the religious habit or some analogous ceremony prescribed by the constitution of the institute. Having attained this status, the novice is immediately under the authority of the local Superior, and, like the postulant, is also a subject of the religious Ordinary's jurisdictional power.[291]

issuing the penal remedies of the Code. They must be either an Ordinary or a Judge.

It is the opinion of the present writer that this confusion may be dispelled by distinguishing between the penal remedies of the Code and the penal remedies which are specified in the Constitutions of the various religious institutes. The penal remedies of the Code are canonical measures which are imposed by those public officials of the Church who are specified in the Code as able to do so, i. e., Ordinaries and Judges. On the other hand, the penal remedies of various religious Constitutions are disciplinary measures which are similar, but only *analogous* to the penal remedies of the Code; and may be imposed by the various Superiors enpowered to do so by their Constitution. While the results of each may be equally effective upon the persons to whom they are given, only the former are official ecclesiastical punishments for ecclesiastical delinquents, the latter are not.

This dissertation considers only the penal remedies of the Code.

288 Cf. Wernz-Vidal, *Ius Canonicum ad Codicis Normam Exactum* (7 vols. in 8, Vol. III., *De Religiosis*, Romae: Societa Tipografica A. Macioce & Pisani, 1933), III, 86, n. 93 [hereafter cited *Ius Canonicum*].

289 Fanfani, *De Iure Religiosorum* (Ed. altera revisa atque notabiliter aucta, Taurini: Marietti, 1925), p. 213, n. 190.

290 Cf. O'Brien, *The Provincial Religious Superior*, p. 86.

291 Cf. O'Brien, *The Provincial Religious Superior*, p. 91.

By reason of their status in an exempt clerical institute, therefore, the postulant and the novice become subjects of the Superiors of the institute and are subject to their exercise of jurisdiction in both the internal and external forum.[292] Those Superiors who are Ordinaries may include the proper use of the penal remedies of the Code in their direction and correction of the postulants and novices.

Furthermore, by extensive force of the constitutions of a particular society, others may also acquire a status whereby they are subject to a religious Ordinary through a juridic relationship.[293] Thus, by approval of the Holy See, a society of nuns may be placed under the jurisdiction of a Regular Superior.[294] In such a case, the Ordinary's jurisdiction might extend to correction and the use of the penal remedies, when such action is permitted by the constitution of the nuns' institute.

Section H. Maintenance of Order in the Society of the Church

The Catholic Church is a society. It consists in a community of members who are united in striving to achieve a common purpose by employing means which are available and common to all.[295] It is a society which is both public and supernatural, having been instituted so that men, as individuals and as members of domestic and civil society may strive for christian perfection in this world and thereby achieve eternal salvation.[296]

A delict, on the other hand, interferes with the social order of the Church.[297] Anyone who commits a delict is responsible for upsetting the order which should exist between man and God, and the order which should also exist among the members of the society of the Church. The misconduct of the delinquent not only inter-

292 *Ad mentem* c. 501, § 1.

293 Cf. Roelker, *Precepts*, p. 62.

294 Cf. c. 500, § 2.

295 The concept of society is adapted from the explanation of Ottaviani, *Institutiones Iuris Publici Ecclesiastici* (3. ed., 2 vols., [Vatican City:] Typis Polyglottis Vaticanis, 1947), I, 33, n. 15 [hereafter cited *Iuris Publici*].

296 Ottaviani, *Iuris Publici*, I, 165.

297 Cf. Regatillo, *Institutiones*, II, 440, n. 776; 441, n. 778.

feres with the attainment of the purpose of the Church in his regard, but it may also lead others astray and further thwart the harmony and order which should characterize the Church as a society.

The Church, furtherfore, as a juridically perfect society possesses the right to all the means which are necessary to achieve its God-given purpose.[298] To attain this purpose, the Church employs the legislative power to properly guide its members, and its coactive power and penal law with the twofold objective of preventing the violation of order through deterrents from crime and repairing the violation of order by punishments for crimes already committed.[299] Thus through its penal law, the Church strives to employ those legitimate means [300] which the lawgiver considers to be necessary for the preservation of its order as a society.[301]

As an approved group of ecclesiastical punishments, the penal remedies share in this objective of the Church's penal law to safeguard the social order of the Church. Indeed, their chief objective, as has been previously noted, is the prevention of delicts and the consequent elimination of the scandal and disturbance of order which accompanies delicts.[302] Because of this objective, the definition of penal remedies should signify that they are *to maintain order in the society of the Church.*

Definition

A consideration of the characteristics of the penal remedies of the Code suggests that they may be defined as follows:

> **Moderate canonical measures of penal character, preventive or preventive-repressive in nature, which are employed for cases specified by law and imposed by a competent authority upon members of the Church to maintain its social order.**

298 Cf. Ottaviani, *Iuris Publici*, I, 53; 157-158.

299 Cf. Sipos, *Enchiridion*, p. 807; Beste, *Introductio*, p. 960; Cocchi, *Commentarium*, VIII, 43, n. 20.

300 Cf. c. 2214, § 1.

301 Cf. Casey, *A Study of Canon 2222, § 1*, The Catholic University of America Canon Law Studies, n. 290 (Washington, D. C.: The Catholic University of America Press, 1949), p. 31.

302 Cf. cc. 2307; 2308 *et al.*

CHAPTER III

THE PENALITY OF THE PENAL REMEDIES

A study of the penal remedies of the code prompts the inquiry: "Are these penal remedies true ecclesiastical penalties in the strict juridic sense of the term?"[1] This is indeed a basic question and merits to be considered at this time.

Article I. An Evaluation of Some Reasons for Considering the Penal Remedies to be True Penalties

When the position and use of the penal remedies of the Code are studied carefully, some reasons suggest themselves for holding the view that they are true ecclesiastical penalties. Among these reasons the following may be listed as deserving one's attention:

1. The penal remedies are presented in Book V of the Code and are thus presumed to be penal in character, since Book V is that section of the Code which deals with the penal law of the Church. This presumption seems to be increased when one realizes that the penal remedies are referred to in Title IV of Book V, which treats *De poenarum notione, speciebus, interpretatione atque applicatione.*

2. They are called *penal* remedies. Why call them *penal* if they are not penalties?

3. The penal remedies may be used at times as substitutes for the true penalties prescribed in the Code. They must, therefore, be penalties themselves.

4. The penal remedies are used as official means for correcting delinquents (c. 2216); therefore they must be penalties.

5. The penal remedies are prescribed only for cases which involve a certain delict, or a well-founded suspicion that a true delict has been committed; or for cases in which, although the

[1] A consideration of the notion of an ecclesiastical penalty is given in Article II of this chapter.

action has not yet occurred, it would be a true delict if it is allowed to be committed; or for cases of scandal or grave disturbance of order. Because of their relationship with delicts, the penal remedies must be penalties.

6. The imposition of the penal remedies of the Code is limited to Ordinaries and ecclesiastical Judges. Both of these officials have the exercise of the power of jurisdiction by reason of their office. Since only those possessing jurisdiction can inflict ecclesiastical penalties, the penal remedies must be penalties.

At first glance, it may be granted that these views, especially in their cumulative effect, have some cogency. They must therefore be examined more closely in order to determine whether or not these remedies are true penalties.

1. The fact that the penal remedies are in Book V of the Code leads one to presume that they are penalties, the same as suspension, excommunication, interdict, etc. This presumption, however, readily admits of proof to the contrary. It cannot be denied that if the penal remedies do not measure up to the full requirements of a true penalty as defined by the Code, then the fact that they are in Book V would not thereby make them penalties.

Their presence in the Fifth Book could be explained by the equally valid reason that, while they are not true penalties, they nevertheless are so closely allied with penalties that the legislator considered Book V to be the best place to present them. The pattern would thus consist in first presenting the true penalties, and then in subjoining immediately those punishments which, though not completely qualified, still come very close to possessing the full requirements of a true penalty. This latter explanation seems very plausable when one realizes that penances are also included in this section of the Code. Penances are usually considered not to be penalties, but rather to be laborious works which are voluntarily accepted by a delinquent so that he may escape a true penalty or obtain absolution or dispensation from a penalty which he has already contracted.[2]

Moreover, the fact that the penal remedies are included under the title *De poenarum notione, speciebus, interpretatione atque*

[2] Cf. Regatillo, *Institutiones*, II, 471, n. 833.

applicatione does not give conclusive proof that they are penalties. The word *poena* may also be understood here as the more generic term meaning punishment. The title could thus refer to the notion, species, interpretation and application of ecclesiastical punishments, and could include methods of discipline and correction other than those which are comprehended in the more limited term of true ecclesiastical penalty.

2. It is true that they are called *penal* remedies. It is likewise true that this is a strong reason for presuming that they are true penalties. *Penal* is indeed part of their official name. As stated above, however, they must fit the Code's pattern of a penalty before they may be properly called true ecclesiastical penalties. Even if they fall short of the requirements for a true penalty, there might be a sound basis for calling them penal.

While not admitting that they are true penalties, the authors present several reasons for calling these remedies *penal.* According to Ayrinhac-Lydon, the penal remedies are so closely associated with penalties that they are said to partake of the nature of a punishment,[3] even though they lack some requirements of a true penalty. Coronata considers these remedies to be penal norms because they have the characteristic of *penality* or penalty-ness about them.[4] DeMeester [5] and Wernz [6] concur with this opinion that the penal remedies have a characteristic which may best be described as penality.

In what then would this penality which is suggested by the authors consist? Blat says that they are penal because they bring to their subject some kind of indisposition.[7] Ayrinhac-Lydon believes that due to the circumstances in which they are applied, the penal remedies are painful to human feelings, and indeed a punishment to the person upon whom they are inflicted.[8] According to Coronata, the penal remedies agree with penalties, at least in

[3] Cf. Penal Legislation, p. 134, n. 176.

[4] Cf. *Institutiones*, IV, 281, n. 1838. Present writer supplied italics.

[5] *Compendium*, p. 228, n. 1800.

[6] *Ius Decretalium*, VI, 258, n. 253.

[7] *Commentarium*, V, 188, n. 139.

[8] *Penal Legislation*, p. 134, n. 176.

the following points: 1) they are imposed for a fault or a grave suspicion that a delict has been committed; therefore they have some connection with a delict; 2) they are given by a Superior; 3) they injure somewhat the reputation of the one upon whom they are inflicted.[9] Cocchi [10] and Wernz [11] consider the remedies to be penal because they convey some lessening of esteem and some annoyance upon the person to whom they are applied. Roelker cites Chelodi also to the effect that these penal remedies approximate penalties because they carry some dishonor with them.[12]

Thus from these various points of view of the authors, the same conclusion is reached. The penal remedies could be properly named even though they did not fulfill the canonical definition of a true penalty. In so far as they have a strong characteristic of penality or penalty-ness, they may be termed penal. They are remedies which have penality.

3. Penal remedies are used as substitutes for penalties.[13] They are also used to diminish or increase a penalty.[14] However, the fact that they are employed in these various ways would not, of itself, mean that the penal remedies are penalties. Here again, it must be demanded that they may not be called ecclesiastical penalties unless they possess the requirements of the definition of the Code. In the event that they fall short of the mark and do not have all of these requirements, then they must not be termed penalties but rather canonical measures having penality, which are employed to substitute for, modify or increase a true penalty.

Regatillo explains that in some cases they are penal *remedies* in the extent that they are used to remedy a prescribed penalty in order to make it more equitable or effective. They remedy a penalty.[15]

By the use of such measures, the legislator has placed in the hands of the Ordinary or judge a freedom of decision and more

[9] *Institutiones*, IV, 79, n. 1689.

[10] *Commentarium*, VIII, 207, n. 120.

[11] *Ius Decretalium*, VI, 258, n. 253.

[12] *Precepts*, p. 192.

[13] Cf. e. g., c. 1947.

[14] Cf. Chapter II, pp. 47, 50.

[15] Cf. *Institutiones*, II, 531, n. 957.

adequate method of punishment which may best serve the interest of justice. The power of their office is not intended primarily for punishing the commission of a delict to the strict letter of the law, but according to canonical equity.[16]

When considered as a remedy for a penalty, the title penal remedy cannot be seen to consist of two separate and independent entities. Rather the term is to be accepted as a composite entity in which each element (penal and remedy) is a qualification of the other, and neither is considered to stand alone or to be the principal element.

If the Oridinary can issue a penalty, then in view of circumstances involved, the legislator gives him the like power to give some punishment which is less than a penalty. This is an exemplification of the Rules of Law: *Plus semper in se continet quod est minus*:[17] and, *Cui licet quod est plus, licet utique quod est minus.*[18]

When the penal remedies are added to penalties they are thus used because of their preventive or preventive-repressive value to safeguard against the recurrence of the delicts. The legislator has foreseen that, in this way, the order of the society is best maintained. The fact, however, that they are added to true penalties would not of itself make these penal remedies also penalties in turn. They could be less than true penalties, or involve no penality at all, and still serve the purpose for which they are added.

4. In canon 2216 one reads:

> *In Ecclesia delinquentes plectuntur:*
> *1° Poenis medicinalibus seu censuris;*
> *2° Poenis vindicativis;*
> *3° Remediis poenalibus et poenitentiis.*

At first glance, it seems that all of these means of punishment are of equal status before the law. While they are apparently different in species, they nevertheless seem to be classified in such a way that one is considered to be equal to the others in fulfilling

[16] Cf. Cocchi, *Commentarium*, VIII, 57, n. 34.

[17] Reg. 35, R. J. in VI°—Bartoccetti, *De Regulis Iuris Canonici* (Roma: Belardetti, 1955), pp. 145-148.

[18] Reg. 53, R. J. in VI°.—Bartoccetti, *De Regulis Iuris Canonici*, pp. 192-193.

the notion of a penalty. Each appears to be a penalty, having its own specific difference or point of view.

Upon closer examination, however, it becomes apparent that here, too, the terminology has been so well chosen that it is broad enough to include the penal remedies within the categories of the canon even though they are or are not true penalties. The verb *plectuntur* signifies punishment and could certainly include a broader concept of punishments than that of the ecclessiastical penalties in the strict sense. The canon reads, "In the Church delinquents are punished . . ." and then ennumerates the various methods. There is really no indication that these methods all have the same characteristic of being true penalties. Various methods of punishment are merely listed. There would be no validity in the position that, since penal remedies are official methods of punishment, they must therefore possess all the basic characteristics of all the other methods. Canon 2216 presents a generic list of canonical methods of punishing delinquents in the Church. Their common-denominator is the fact that each is a method of punishing delinquents. Nothing more is stated, and therefore nothing more can be claimed. One must look beyond this canon to determine whether or not the penal remedies are truly penalties.[19]

5. An examination of the prescriptions of the Code clearly reveals that the penal remedies are used only in cases where a true delict, or well-founded suspicion of the existence of a true delict, or conduct which would lead to a true delict are involved. From this fact, however, it does not necessarily follow that every method for preventing or correcting a delictual situation is *eo ipso facto* a true penalty. All penalties are methods for correcting delicts; but all methods for correcting delicts need not necessarily be penalties. Lesser measures of punishment may also be used when such action is prescribed or permitted by law. This procedure is a valid use of the Rule of Law which was previously cited: *Cui licet quod est plus, licet utique quod est minus.*[20]

[19] The fact, as stated by c. 2216, that the penal remedies are methods of punishing delinquents is verified by other canons which are considered in this thesis, e.g. cc. 2308; 2310; 2311; 1933, § 4; 2223, § 3, 3°; 2224, § 2; 2234. The law also makes provision, over and above the contents of c. 2216, for handling potential delinquents, e.g. cc. 2307; 2309.

[20] Reg. 53, R. J. in VI°.—Bartoccetti, *De Regulis Iuris Canonici*, pp. 192-193.

6. The Penal Remedies of the Code can only be imposed by an Ordinary [21] or by a judge when he is presiding in tribunal.[22] While it is true that these persons whom the law specifies as being capable of imposing the penal remedies are actually persons who do possess jurisdiction,[23] this fact would not be conclusive evidence that the remedies are true penalties. Certainly not all acts of discipline and punishment which are permitted or indeed provided by law to be employed by the Ordinary or judge may be concluded to be, by that very fact, true ecclesiastical penalties. One must look not only to the quality of the person who imposes them, but also, as has been previously considered, to the pattern set by the definition of the Code, before it can be concluded that the penal remedies are true ecclesiastical penalties.

None of the preceding views establish the fact that the penal remedies are penalties. Their value, whether considered singly or in their cumulative effect, could serve, at most, to supplement the fact that they are penalties, once it has been proven. In the last analysis the penal remedies may be called penalties only if they meet the requirements for a penalty as specified by the Code in its definition. What then are these requirements?

Article II. The Canonical Concept of Ecclesiastical Penalties

The Code defines an ecclesiastical penalty as the privation of some good, inflicted by legitimate authority, for the correction of delinquents and as punishment for a delict.[24] This definition contains three distinct elements: 1) An evil, 2) An authority and 3) A purpose.[25]

Section A. The Privation of Some Good (i. e. An Evil)

All penalties in general contain some element of evil. This evil results from suffering or enduring something, or from being de-

[21] Cf. c. 2307; c. 2308; c. 2311.

[22] C. 2309, § 3; c. 2223, § 3, 3°.

[23] Cf. Roelker, *Precepts*, p. 44.

[24] C. 2215: Poena ecclesiastica est privatio alicuius boni ad delinquentis correctionem et delicti punitionem a legitima auctoritate inflicta.

[25] Cf. Regatillo, *Institutiones*, II, 470, n. 830: *malum, finis, auctoritas.*

prived of something, as punishment for committing a delict. Thus, Wernz defines penalties in general as being that evil of suffering or of privation which is justly inflicted by a legitimate authority because of a delict, so that the social order might be preserved; and inflicted even upon those who are unwilling to accept it.[26]

Today the element of evil which is contained in ecclesiastical penalties is based upon the privation of some good, rather than the enduring of some suffering. If there is any evil of suffering in ecclesiastical penalties, this is rather the result of, or the accompaniment of the privation of some good rather than the direct objective of the penalty. Such suffering could consist in both the mental and physical reactions which result from being deprived of some good. There may also be the psychic and moral sufferings of embarrassment, shame and sense of dishonor which may result from the same privation. Regardless of the fact that the delinquent does or does not endure such suffering, however, the current mind of the Church is that the cause of justice is best served when, in order to counteract the evil of a delict, there is a corresponding evil of a penalty consisting in the privation of some good.[27]

The goods which the Church deprives Her subjects are certain rights and goods given either by nature, by Christ, or instituted by the Church, and which have been left to the Church's administration with the authority of conceding them or taking them away.[28] These goods may be either material or spiritual [29] and may include: the administration or reception of the sacraments, assistance at Mass, indulgences, the right of patronage, freedom, one's good name and reputation, temporal goods, honors, etc.[30] Their scope would not extend, however, to areas dealing with the intimate conditions of a person's soul, e. g. the sacramental character, the ability to perform a meritorious act, or the state of sanctifying grace.[31]

26 *Ius Decretalium*, VI, 79, n. 71.

27 Cf. Cocchi, *Commentarium*, VIII, 43, n. 20.

28 Cf. DeMeester, *Compendium*, p. 138, n. 1707; Vermeersch-Creusen, *Epitome*, III, 237, n. 403.

29 Coronata, *Institutiones*, IV, 74, n. 1688.

30 Cf. Vermeersch-Creusen, *Epitome*, III, 237, n. 403; DeMeester, *Compendium*, p. 138, n. 1707.

31 DeMeester, *Compendium*, p. 138, n. 1707.

SECTION B. INFLICTED BY LEGITIMATE AUTHORITY

Not every authority in the Church may impose or inflict ecclesiastical penalties. This power is reserved to those who are specified by law to do so, and the term *a legitima auctoritate inflicta* refers only to an ecclesiastical superior having the power to determine penalties.[32]

The power to inflict a penalty involves the evercise of the power of jurisdiction.[33] This ability must be clearly distinguished from a disciplinary sanction imposed by an official of an imperfect society. There are many societies in the Church which lack the power of jurisdiction, and are incapable of possessing it, e. g. associations of the laity and congregations of religious women. There are other societies which are capable of possessing it, by concession of the Roman Pontiff, but as a matter of fact do not possess it, e. g. some non-exempt clerical institutes. All of these societies, however, by reason of dominative and domestic power, are able to impose disciplinary sanctions upon their members for the purpose of safeguarding the observance of their rule.[34] Superiors of these societies do not possess legitimate authority to inflict ecclesiastical penalties (e. g. suspension, excommunication, etc.). At most, they are able to demand a fulfillment of the law of the Church, or the completing of an agreement made by reason of association with the society, e. g. to observe their vows and the rule of the community, by reason of the vows pronounced.[35] In effect then, these superiors may impose reasonable and just sanctions which may affect a member's status in the particular society; but they cannot impose ecclesiastical penalties, as public officials in the Church, which affect the member's status in the Church.

Ecclesiastical penalties may be inflicted only by those who are specified by the law as being legitimately empowered to do so. The Code clearly states that whoever has the power of making laws or imposing precepts is also able to attach penalties to the law or precept; while those who have only judicial power, are only

[32] Cocchi, *Commentarium*, VIII, 43, n. 20.

[33] Regatillo, *Institutiones*, II, 471, n. 832.

[34] Regatillo, *ibid.*

[35] Cf. Vermeersch-Creusen, *Epitome*, III, 237, n. 403.

able to apply penalties of legitimate statutes according to the norms of law.[36] Unless he has a special mandate, the Vicar General does not share in this power to inflict penalties.[37] Therefore the only authorities of the Church who may legitimately inflict penalties are those who possess the exercise of legislative or judicial power of jurisdiction in the external forum; and furthermore, these authorities are limited in so far as they may exercise their power only within the framework of the provisions or norms of law.

SECTION C. CORRECTION OF THE DELINQUENT AND AS PUNISHMENT FOR A DELICT (i. e. A PURPOSE)

The foundation of the punitive power in the Church rests upon the primary necessity of safeguarding the order of its society. Indeed the Church cannot withdraw from this objective of its penal law because this function is essentially the purpose of all criminal justice and all punitive power.[38]

Penalty is the reaction of order against disorder.[39] The threat of a penalty safeguards order, lest it be broken; and the imposition of a penalty repairs a breach of order. For this reason, Regatillo states that the vindictive aspect, the safeguarding of the social order by punishing for the commission of a delict, is always present in some measure or other in every penalty.[40]

Although the Church is an institute for the salvation of souls, it is nonetheless a social institute, existing primarily and *per se* for all its members and not primarily for any individual member. In the application of penalties, therefore, even if there were no hope for the reform of a particular delinquent, or on the other hand, even if he has already reformed, the repair of the social order and preservation of justice as an example to others would be reason enough why at least in certain cases, the penalty should be inflicted and not overlooked.[41]

36 Cf. c. 2220, § 1.

37 Cf. c. 2220, § 2.

38 Cf. Cocchi, *Commentarium*, VIII, 43, n. 20; Wernz, *Ius Decretalium*, VI, 81, n. 73.

39 St. Thomas, *Summa Theologia*, $I^{a}II^{ae}$, q. 87, a. 1.

40 Regatillo, *Institutiones*, II, 471, n. 832.

41 Cf. Vermeersch-Creusen, *Epitome*, III, 237, n. 401.

The Church, however, most often does not prescind from the reform of the delinquent[42] but indeed includes the medicinal character in many of its penalties. These medicinal penalties, or those which possess some degree of the medicinal character, are inflicted mostly to reform the delinquent and lead him from evil so that he will faithfully comply with the law. They seek to correct the ill-will or contumacy of the delinquent.[43]

Thus, while exercising Her coercive power to protect and preserve order in Her society, the Church nevertheless is expressly mindful of Her purpose as a society, the salvation of mankind. She is attentive to the spiritual health of the faithful, giving adequate care to their needs as individuals and as a society. Her penalties are both medicinal and vindictive, seeking the "correction of the delinquent and punishment for the delict."[44]

Article III. The Penal Remedies Compared to the Code's Concept of True Ecclesiastical Penalties

As has been seen, the concept for every true ecclesiastical penalty is presented in canon 2215 and consists in three elements: 1) The privation of some good; 2) Inflicted by a legitimate authority; 3) For the correction of the delinquent and as punishment for a delict. If the penal remedies are properly to be called penalties, they must contain all of these three elements. A comparison is in order.

Section A. The Privation of Some Good

Most frequently the penal remedies either impose, repeat, or strengthen the discipline upon a person's conduct relative to his actions, speech, or obligations of state in life.[45] Because of the circumstances of a case, some things or persons must be avoided because they are the proximate occasion of a delict for a certain delinquent, even though such things would be perfectly legitimate for other persons. To this extent at least, therefore, the penal

[42] Cf. Vermeersch-Creusen, *Epitome*, III, 237, n. 403.

[43] Berutti, *Institutiones*, VI, 63.

[44] C. 2215.

[45] Cf. cc. 2306-2311.

remedies carry with them a limitation of liberty. Furthermore, as will be considered in the subsequent chapter, the use of surveillance certainly imposes in varying degrees the evil of a definite curtailment of freedom for the person upon whom it is inflicted.

All of the authors who treat of the matter, moreover, point out that the penal remedies have the character or quality of penality and penalty-ness, because the averting or repressing of a delict is accompanied by some loss of honor of the person to whom they are given.[46] Roelker likewise observes that the penal remedies approximate penalties because they carry with them some dishonor.[47]

Thus, the person's honor, repute, good name, dignity, self respect, esteem, reputation are in some degree lessened by the act of being warned, rebuked, commanded by precept, or made subject to surveillance. Most frequently, of course, these would also be accompanied by a natural sense of shame, hurt feelings and embarrassment. The penal remedies, therefore, from two aspects impose an evil upon the person to whom they are given: they deprive him, in some measure, of the goods of (1) freedom and (2) honor. They thus constitute a *privatio alicuius boni* and possess this element of a penalty.

SECTION B. INFLICTED BY A LEGITIMATE AUTHORITY

Only two classes of persons are named in the Code as being the ones to impose penal remedies: Ordinaries[48] and ecclesiastical judges.[49] The Ordinaries may act personally or through a delegate.[50]

It is evident from canon 2220, § 1 that these persons have legitimate authority to inflict ecclesiastical penalties. It is equally

[46] E. g. Coronata, *Institutiones*, IV, 281, n. 1838; Vermeersch-Creusen, *Epitome*, III, 306, n. 501; Wernz, *Ius Decretalium*, VI, 258, n. 253; Sipos, *Enchiridion*, p. 852.

[47] *Precepts*, p. 192; p. 196.

[48] Cf. cc. 2307; 2308; 2309, § 3; 2311; 1933, § 4; 1947. The Vicar General is excluded unless he has a special mandate—cf. Chapter II, p. 53.

[49] Cf. cc. 2309, § 3; 2223, § 3, 3°; 2224; 2234. The Superior of c. 2309, § 6 is considered by the present writer to be a synonym for Ordinary and judge—cf. Chapter II, p. 61.

[50] Cc. 2307; 2308.

evident, therefore, that the penal remedies possess this second element of a penalty because they qualify as *a legitima auctoritate inflicta.*

SECTION C. CORRECTION OF THE DELINQUENT AND AS PUNISHMENT FOR A DELICT

As as been seen, most authors attribute some penality or penaltyness to the penal remedies because they at least impart some lessening of honor upon the person to whom they are given. Other than this, some do not further consider the possibility whether or not they might be true penalties.

The crux of the question whether or not the penal remedies are penalties lies ultimately in the concepts of delict and delinquent. Penalties are given for the purpose of correcting a delinquent and as a punishment for a delict. What then is a delict? What is a delinquent? May the proximate danger of committing a delict be considered equivalent to a delict itself?

Canon 2195 presents the definition of a delict: "By the word delict in ecclesiastical law, there is understood the external and morally imputable violation of a law to which at least an indetermined canonical sanction has been attached." [51]

The authors point out that the act which constitutes a delict must have been committed before it can actually be considered a delict. A penal law must have been violated; i. e., there must have been an actual violation, not merely the proximate danger of doing so. Coronata points out this position when he states it is apparent that *per se* the penal remedies lack some notion of a penalty given by the Code, because penalties presuppose the existence of a delict.[52] He believes that since these remedies are indeed penal, they suppose at least some guilt and transgression of law, but this transgression does not necessarily pertain to the nature of a delict.[53] Vermeersch-Creusen observe that not all privation of a good is a penalty, but only that which is inflicted as punishment for a delict.[54] They

[51] C. 2195, § 1: Nomine delicti, iure ecclesiastico, intelligitur externa et moraliter imputabilis legis violatio cui addita sit sanctio canonica saltem indeterminata.

[52] *Institutiones*, IV, 79, n. 1689.

[53] *Institutiones*, IV, 281, n. 1838.

[54] *Epitome*, III, 237, n. 403.

would therefore not consider the penal remedies to be penalties in the strict sense.

According to Cocchi, the penal remedies are penal because they convey some lessening of esteem and some annoyance to the person upon whom they are applied. He believes this result is based on the fact that the issuance of a penal remedy supposes some transgression of law which, however, may not extend to the point of being a delict.[55] Sipos also says that they are penal means because they have a penal character in so far as they suppose some transgression of law which does not indeed reach to the degree of a delict. He notes that for the transgressor there is an occasion of danger of committing a true delict or else a suspicion of a delict, and as a result there is scandal to the faithful.[56]

Lega has a more detailed discussion of this matter than most authors. He emphasizes the preventive element of the penal remedies, and observes that in so far as they tend to prevent a delict, they do not have the nature of a penal sanction because a sanction always follows, and never precedes the delict which it is sanctioning.[57] To him the whole problem of the possibility of penal remedies being penalties resolves itself by using the criterion that something cannot be understood as a penalty unless it concerns a delict which has already been committed. A penalty cannot be given for a delict which has not yet been committed.[58]

Although Lega does not mention it, his view, together with those of the authors previously cited, seems to be substantiated by canon 2233, § 1: "No penalty may be inflicted unless it is certainly established that a delict has been committed. . . ."[59] For this reason the penal remedies as *preventive* measures seem to lack the element of a delict which has already been committed, and therefore cannot qualify as true penalties. In like manner, the term *delinquent* would be limited to refer to someone who has already committed a delict. Therefore canon 2215 would not include the

[55] *Commentarium*, VIII, 207, n. 120.

[56] *Enchiridion*, p. 852.

[57] *Praelectiones*, I, 66.

[58] *Praelectiones*, I, 66: . . . nisi agatur de delicto iam patrato.

[59] C. 2233, § 1: Nulla poena infligi potest, nisi certo constet delictum commissum fuisse. . . .

potential delinquent, i. e., one who is in the proximate danger of committing a delict.

On the other hand, when the penal remedies are employed as *repressive* measures, a delict has already been committed. The public rebuke would be such an example. This can be given only to a defendant who has either confessed to or has been convicted of committing a delict.[60] The same may be said of the precept as a penal remedy used when the public rebuke has been found to be useless or is prudently thought to be so.[61] Some of the penal remedies do qualify, therefore, as true penalties, for they are used to repress a true delict, and are used to correct someone who is truly a delinquent.

Even in these cases, however, the use of these repressive measures seems to be based on a preventive motive, to the extent that the penal remedies are employed with the hope and intention of preventing a repetition or recurrence of the delict. Here also the spirit of the law, the *mens ligislatoris* for the interpretation of laws,[62] seems to employ the penal remedy to be more of a remedy for a penalty rather than a true penalty itself. Although a delict has been committed and there is also a privation of some good inflicted by legitimate authority, the penal remedy is used to substitute for, diminish, or increase a penalty rather than to exist as a penalty in its own right. Regatillo, Jone and Coronata concur in this opinion.[63] Roelker seems to allude to this characteristic when he states, "penal remedies are given to prevent crime rather than to punish it." [64]

Mindful of their various uses in the Code, and the opinions of representative authors, the present writer holds that the penal remedies possess a definite characteristic of penality and are very proximate to penalties, but they cannot be considered as true penalties in the strict sense of the definition of canon 2215. At most, it may be said that some of them qualify as true penalties.

[60] Cf. c. 2309, § 3.

[61] C. 2310.

[62] C. 18.

[63] Cf. *Regatillo, Institutiones*, II, 531, n. 957; Jone, *Commentarium*, III, 417; Coronata, *Institutiones*, IV, 281, n. 1838.

[64] *Precepts*, p. 192.

Since some of them do not completely fulfill the definition of an ecclesiastical penalty, however, it must be admitted that, considering the group of penal remedies as a legal entity or canonical institute, they are *ad instar* penal, but are not penalties.

The *penality* which is characteristic of the penal remedies may be attributed to the following facts:

1. They convey a lessening of honor to the person upon whom they are imposed.

2. They are inflicted by legitimate public ecclesiastical authority.

3. Their issuance is intimately connected with grave external faults, delicts, and true penalties, since they are employed as measures to prevent and check delicts and also as means to avert, substitute for, diminish, or increase ecclesiastical penalties.

In addition to their characteristic of penality, they are *remedies*, for they strive to remedy the necessity for, the excessive severity of, or the deficiency of an ecclesiastical penalty.

They are penal remedies because they strive to preserve the health of the society of the Church by: preventing the commission or continuation of delicts, removing the stimuli of scandal together with the voluntary occasions and proximate causes of delinquency.[65]

SCHOLION. COMPARISON OF THE PENAL REMEDIES WITH THE MEDICINAL AND VINDICTIVE PENALTIES

The several officially prescribed methods of punishing delinquents in the Church as listed in canon 2216 [66] differ not only in their penal nature, but are also distinct legal institutes, differing in many characteristics one from the other.

Ultimately, of course, as has been previously noted,[67] the purpose of all penal legislation and coercive power in the Church is to safeguard Her social order, so that the Church may better achieve Her purpose as a society. In this sense, all punishments have the

[65] Cf. *Sacra Haec*, n. 2; DeMeester, *Compendium*, p. 228, n. 1800.

[66] C. 2216: In Ecclesia delinquentes plectuntur:

1.° Poenis medicinalibus seu censuris
2.° Poenis vindicativis
3.° Remediis poenalibus et poenitentiis.

[67] E. g. Chapter II, p. 87.

same ultimate goal. In regard to the individual methods of punishment, however, it is evident that each has a distinct proximate purpose,[68] or purpose which it directly seeks especially to achive [69] in order to attain the ultimate goal. Their individual distinctive point of view or approach to the problem of delinquency, together with other essential characteristics which each possesses, produces a definite specific difference among the medicinal penalties, vindictive penalties, and the penal remedies of the Code. While they are not so mutually exclusive that the phases of one purpose could not, in any given case, be found to be present with another type of punishment, there is nevertheless a clear specific difference among them. These methods of punishment have been compared very well by Coronata [70] and an adaptation of this comparison may be presented as follows:

Medicinal Penalties—

1. Immediately seek to put an end to contumacy and to effect the reform of the delinquent. The emphasis here is upon the welfare of the individual. These punishments look to the cure of a member who is socially errant. Society is benefited by effecting the well-being of its member.

2. May be used only when a true delict has been committed.

3. May be imposed only after the contumacy of the delinquent has been established.

4. Are given for no determined length of time other than the cessation of contumacy.

5. Are removed by absolution.

Vindictive Penalties—

1. Immediately seek to punish for the commission of a delict in order to repair the broken social order by public retribution and to deter others from similar delinquency. The emphasis here is upon expiation for the commission of crime.

[68] Cf. Cocchi, *Commentarium*, VIII, 43, n. 21; DeMeester, *Compendium*, p. 139, n. 1708.

[69] Cf. Berutti, *Institutiones*, VI, 63.

[70] Cf. *Institutiones*, IV, 79, n. 1689.

2. May be used only when a true delict has been committed.

3. May be imposed upon a reformed delinquent as well as upon one who is contumacious.

4. Usually are given for a determined time limit.

5. Cease either by expiration of the time specified for the duration of the penalty, or else they are removed by dispensation.

Penal Remedies—

1. Immediately seek to prevent the commission or repetition of delicts. While neither excluding the reform of the delinquent or the repair of social order, the emphasis here is on adequate crime-prevention.

2. May be imposed, at times, even in the absence of a true delict.

3. While employed primarily for crime-prevention, these and also used to substitute for, diminish, or increase a penalty.

4. May be imposed upon those who are contumacious, and even upon those who are not contumacious.

5. Are not removed by absolution or dispensation but rather are *ex se* perpetual in so far as their obligation lasts as long as the proximate danger of delictual conduct endures, safeguarding the provisions of canon 24.

CHAPTER IV

THE PENAL REMEDIES OF CANON 2306–2311

The purpose of this chapter is to consider the interrelation and application of the specific penal remedies of the Code of Canon Law as indicated in canons 2306-2311.[1]

Article I. An Enumeration of the Penal Remedies of the Code

Canon 2306 presents an official list of the penal remedies of the Code: [2]

The penal remedies are:

1. Warning
2. Rebuke
3. Precept
4. Surveillance

In this listing there are both similarities and differences in respect to the canonical remedies of the pre-Code legislation of *Sacra Haec*

[1] As was noted in the Foreword, it is beyond the scope of this present work to enter into an exhaustive study of any specific penal remedy, giving a detailed consideration of the various phases of its application throughout the Code. It is thought that such a study of warning, rebuke, or surveillance might constitute the purview of other dissertations in this series of Canon Law Studies. The excellent publications: *The Particular Penal Precept* by H. G. Quinn (The Catholic University of America Canon Law Studies n. 303, 1953), and *Precepts* by the late Dean of the School of Canon Law at the Catholic University of America, Right Reverend Monsignor Edward Roelker (St. Anthony Guild Press, 1955), have already given adequate consideration to the precept and its uses. This present dissertation strives to present the canonical concept of the penal remedies in general together with a study of the application of canons 2306-2311.

[2] Remedia poenalia sunt:

1.° Monitio
2.° Correptio
3.° Praeceptum
4.° Vigilantia

and *Cum Magnopere.*[3] The chief similarity lies in the fact that the general characteristic of being moderate canonical measures of discipline is maintained. Then, too, the use of the warning and the precept is prescribed in the law of both eras.[4] The Code introduced an evident departure from the former legislation by the addition of the rebuke and surveillance as penal remedies, and the transfer of spiritual exercises from the status of preservative or preventive remedy [5] to one of the penances of the Code.[6] Moreover, the pre-Code legislation gave apparent indication by the use of the term *praecipue* that the list of the remedies was demonstrative. There is no such indication in the Code.[7]

SECTION A. THE HIERARCHY OF THE PENAL REMEDIES

In the list of the penal remedies there is a gradation or hierarchy of arrangement according to their relative severity: first the warning or rebuke depending upon the presence of the circumstances prescribed for their use,[8] or else the warning followed when necessary by the rebuke in cases involving delicts which are certain, then the more severe precept, and finally surveillance.[9] Roelker notes that apparently the penal remedies of the Code are not to be used indiscriminately, but gradually, according to their need.[10] This statement seems verified by canon 2310, which provides that the precept is to be used subsequently to the decision that the warning and rebuke either have been given to no avail, or when conditions indicate that their issuance would be hopelessly ineffective.

Normally then, the proper use of the penal remedies calls for the issuance of the lesser ones first, followed by the more severe

[3] Cf. *Sacra Haec,* nn. 1-9; *Cum Magnopere,* nn. I-IX; cc. 2306-2311.

[4] Cf. *Sacra Haec,* n. 4; *Cum Magnopere,* n. IV; c. 2306.

[5] *Sacra Haec,* n. 4; Cum Magnopere, n. IV.

[6] C. 2313, 5°.

[7] Compare c. 2306 with *Sacra Haec,* n. 4 and *Cum Magnopere,* n. IV.

[8] Cf. cc. 2307 and 2308.

[9] In the pre-Code legislation, there was no indication where the spiritual exercises had place in the application of the remedies. It was clear, however, that warnings were to precede the use of precepts.—Cf. *Sacra Haec,* n. 7.

[10] *Precepts,* p. 194.

remedies, if the proper conditions for using the latter are present and the need persists. When the gravity or urgency of a particular case would require it, however, the preliminary use of the lesser remedy need not be followed as long as the canonical conditions for using the more severe remedy are present. Accordingly, Blat observes that the provision of *Sacra Haec* that the application of the remedies is left to the conscience and prudenec of the Ordinaries, guided by the prescripts of the canons and the accompanying gravity of the case, is similarly provided for by the Code today.[11]

SECTION B. AN EXCLUSIVE LIST

Canon 2306 contains no explicit indication that it presents either an exclusive or a demonstrative list. When the penal remedies are prescribed to be used, therefore, there is a question whether the Ordinary may employ only those remedies which are listed, or whether similar and at least equally effective measures may also be used as penal remedies for such cases.

As has been previously noted in this chapter, no such problem resulted from the pre-Code legislation. Both *Sacra Haec* and *Cum Magnopere* clearly state that the preservative or preventive remedies are especially thought to be spiritual exercises, warnings and precepts.[12] Thus, these Instructions patently contain a demonstrative list. The authors seem to agree unanimously that there is no intention in these Instructions to present an exhaustive or exclusive enumeration, or to limit the resourcefulness of the Ordinary in his exercise of these disciplinary measures.[13] The qualification resulting from the use of the term *praecipue* left ample freedom of choice to the Ordinary if he prudently and conscientiously decided to employ some other measure as a canonical remedy.

There is, however, no use of *praecipue* or any other qualification

[11] Cf. *Commentarium*, V, 190, n. 143; *Sacra Haec*, n. 3.

[12] *Sacra Haec*, n. 4: Mediis, quae praeservant, praecipue accensentur spiritualia exercitia, monitiones et praecepta; *Cum Magnopere*, n. IV: Praeventiva remedia sunt praecipue spiritualia exercitia, monitiones, praecepta.

[13] Cf. Lega, *Praelectiones*, IV, 351, n. 281; Wernz, *Ius Decretalium*, VI, 259, n. 253; Berutti, *Institutiones*, VI, 239, n. 93.

in canon 2306. As a result, the authors seem to be rather equally divided in their opinions that this is or is not an exclusive list. Ayrinhac-Lydon present the poblem but offer no solution to it at all.[14] The other authors who consider the matter do take a position on it. While offering no reason for his view, Coronata states that the enumeration seems to be demonstrative rather than all-inclusive.[15] Likewise, Vermeersch-Creusen say that the remedies which are listed in canon 2306 are given as examples, and are not proposed as a closed or completed list.[16] Most likely these authors are relying to a great extent on the pre-Code legislation as a pattern for the present law. There is, moreover, an instance in the Code where it is not clear that the further use of the remedies of canon 2306 would be of much efficacy; but that other measures might serve the purpose. The suggestion here seems to be that there are remedies other than those of canon 2306. Thus canon 661, § 1 states that to the warnings (which are really precepts)[17] given to a recalcitrant religious, should be added exhortations, corrections, penances, and *penal remedies* which are considered apt for the reform of the delinquent and for the repair of scandal. Except for surveillance, it is difficult to imagine what other penal remedies of canon 2306 might be effective here, whereas some other conceivable measure might achieve the desired results. Whatever their reasoning, these authors hold that the list of canon 2306 is merely demonstrative of the measures which may be employed when the use of the penal remedies is prescribed.

On the other hand, both Blat[18] and Berutti[19] maintain the position that the penal remedies which are enumerated in canon 2306 constitute a strictly exclusive list. The present writer agrees with the opinions of these latter authors. This position is based on the fact that the text of canon 2306 lists the penal remedies as warning, rebuke, precept, and surveillance, with no indication that

14 Cf. *Penal Legislation*, p. 135-136.

15 Cf. *Institutiones*, IV, 282, n. 1839.

16 *Epitome*, III, 306, n. 501.

17 Cf. c. 661, § 3: Singulis monitionibus adiiciatur dimissionis comminatio.

18 Cf. *Commentarium*, V, 189, n. 140.

19 *Institutiones*, VI, 239, n. 93.

other measures may share in this classification. There is no use of *praecipue* or similar qualifying term which would point to a possible extension of choice. Since the penal remedies do have the characteristic of penality or of being *ad instar* penal,[20] they are odious to the person upon whom they are imposed. On the basis of the rule *odia restringi,*[21] it seems that the enumeration of canon 2306 must be taken as an exclusive list. Nor would the fact that the pre-Code list of preventive remedies was demonstrative seem to alter this position. Since canon 2306 does not contain *praecipue,* there is a discrepancy with the pre-Code law, and thus the canon should not be understood to conform to the old law on this point, but must be interpreted according to the meaning of the words employed in the canon.[22] This opinion, it should be clearly understood, does not deny the merits of other methods of discipline. It is readily conceded that the Ordinary has an ample variety of measures by which he may effectively prevent the commission of delicts and effect the wise adjustment of a delinquent's scale of values. This opinion does affirm, however, that when the use of the penal remedies is prescribed by law, only those measures which are enumerated in the text of canon 2306 may be so employed.

Article II. The Summary Investigation

Before the penal remedies are employed, a case which involves the possible use of such measures must in some way or other, of course, be brought to the attention of the competent Ordinary. Such a situation may become known as a result of a canonical visitation or other personal experience of the Ordinary. Information may also come to the Ordinary through a report of what is public knowledge or widespread rumor, or by means of denunciation, accusation, bad reputation of the person, oral or written communication or similar sources of information.[23]

The source of such information must indeed be carefully con-

20 Cf. Chapter III, p. 103.

21 Reg. 15, R. J. in VI°.

22 C. 6, 3°: Canones qui ex parte tantum cum veteri iure congruunt . . . qua discrepant, sunt ex sua ipsorum sententia diiudicandi.

23 Cf. Coronata, *Institutiones*, IV, 285, n. 1842; Lega, *Praelectiones*, IV, 350, n. 280.

sidered by the Ordinary. Normally no attention should be paid to denunciations which come from a manifest enemy of the person. Nor should credence be given to information from disreputable and unworthy persons or from anonymous letters which lack the elements and qualities which make an accusation probable.[24] *Per se,* anonymous letters beget no faith as proof.[25] Coronata notes, however, that if they contain specific facts concerning definite times, places, persons and other detailed circumstances, these anonymous letters are not to be *a priori* discarded, but should be used to institute an investigation, in the same manner as would be done when a letter contains an illegible signature.[26]

Once the possibility of delinquency, scandal, disturbance of public order or similar sources of discord in the social order of the Church becomes known to the Ordinary, he has the pastoral obligation of taking proper action.[27]

Unless the circumstances which would warrant the use of the penal remedies are notorious or known certainly to exist by the Ordinary, he must institute a preliminary summary investigation of the matter.[28] The cause of justice requires such action, of course, lest a person be subjected to correction or punishment without foundation.

For the use of the penal remedies, an extra-judicial investigation will often be necessary and sufficient.[29] Such an investigation may be general i. e., directed towards a certain crime, but no definite person; or else against a determined person, but in regard to no particular crime. Most often, however, it will be special, i. e., directed against a definite person and also concern some definite crime.[30]

By all means this investigation must be accomplained by strict secrecy and great caution in order to protect the good name of the person being investigated, and to prevent the rumor of a delict

24 C. 1942, § 2.

25 S. C. S. Off., instr. 20 febr. 1866—*Fontes*, IV, 990, 6.

26 *Institutiones*, IV, 446, n. 1462; also Augustine, *Commentary*, VII, 370.

27 *Ad mentem* cc. 335, § 1; 336, §§ 1, 2.

28 Cf. c. 1939; Wernz, *Ius Decretalium*, VI, 259, n. 254.

29 Coronata, *Institutiones*, III, 444, n. 1461.

30 Cf. De Meester, *Compendium*, p. 229, n. 1804.

from spreading.[31] Special care must also be exercised to protect the reputation of other persons who may be involved in the case.

The Ordinary may conduct the investigation personally. Sometimes, indeed, the circumstances of person or fact may seem to require and militate for such personal action.[32] In general, however, the mind of the law prefers that the investigation should rather be done by a competent, prudent and trustworthy delegate of the Ordinary who is appointed for a specific case.[33]

If the nature of the case requires information from other persons, their assistance may be sought, taking care that their testimony is safeguarded by an oath both to speak the truth and to observe strict secrecy in the matter.[34] This provision allows for the use of witnesses and experts whenever they are considered to be necessary.[35] When testimony is sought from witnesses, the further specification of canon 1944, § 2 and 1772 that the witnesses must be heard individually is to be followed. Since the use of witnesses or experts increases the danger of the investigation resulting in damaged reputations and scandal, the number of persons who are brought into contact with the case should be limited to the minimum found necessary to establish moral certainty of the presence or absence of the conditions required for issuing the various penal remedies.

The findings of the investigation should be put in writing.[36] If the person is found to be innocent, or there is insufficient proof to warrant any disciplinary action against him, these facts should be noted on the record of the investigation and preserved in the secret archives.[37] On the other hand, if there are sufficient grounds for giving one or other of the penal remedies, this also should be noted on the record of the investigation and kept in the secret archives.[38]

[31] C. 1943.

[32] Cf. c. 1940.

[33] Cf. cc. 1940; 1941.

[34] C. 1944.

[35] Coronata, *Institutiones*, III, 449, n. 1694.

[36] Blat, *Commentarium*, V, 190, n. 143; Lega, *Praelectiones*, VI, 349-350, n. 279; Wernz, *Ius Decretalium*, VI, 259, n. 254.

[37] C. 1946; Coronata, *Institutiones*, III, 452, n. 1465.

[38] Coronata, *Institutiones*, III, 452, n. 1465.

This record of the investigation serves the useful purpose of crystalizing the matter. It removes the innocent from the cloud of suspicion. At the same time, if the facts were inconclusive, and the person remains under suspicion, the information may be helpful to subsequent investigations in case there are subsequent accusations of crime. When disciplinary action is necessary, the record points to the fact that such action is just and well-founded, and likewise provides a basis for subsequent action in the event that the matter must be pressed further. In the event that the corrected person seeks legitimate recourse to a higher authority, the record may be used by the Ordinary to give an account of the means he employed and the reasonableness of his actions in regard to the delinquent.[39]

The summary investigation having been completed, the applicaption of the proper penal remedy for the various prescribed cases is left to the prudence and conscience of the Ordinary.

Article III. The Warning (*Monitio*)

The authors vary somewhat in their definition of the warning. They speak of this penal remedy as being an exhortation and advice,[40] a request,[41] a reminder,[42] a reproach,[43] a warning,[44] a calling attention to[45] or pointing out,[46] a striving to reach the mind of a subject,[47] in order to advert to a danger and indicate what is to be done or avoided in his manner of acting. Although differing in their terminology, the views of these authors indicate the

[39] *Lega, Praelectiones*, IV, 350, n. 279; DeMeester, *Compendium*, p. 229, n. 1804; Jone, *Commentarium*, III, 491; Vermeersch-Creusen, *Epitome*, III, 307, n. 503; Coronata, *Institutiones*, IV, 285, n. 1842; *Sacra Haec*, n. 5; Conc. Pl. Balt. III., n. 308.

[40] Berutti, *Institutiones*, VI, 239, n. 94.

[41] Coronata, *Institutiones*, IV, 282, n. 1840.

[42] Regatillo, *Institutiones*, II, 532, n. 958.

[43] Blat, *Commentarium*, V, 189, n. 140; Cocchi, *Commentarium*, VIII, 208, n. 122; Regatillo, *Institutiones*, II, 532, n. 958; Berutti, *Institutiones*, VI, 239, n. 94.

[44] DeMeester, *Compendium*, p. 228, n. 1802.

[45] Vermeersch-Creusen, *Epitome*, III, 307, n. 502.

[46] Sipos, *Enchiridion*, p. 852.

[47] Jone, *Commentarium*, III, 491.

essential concept of this remedy. Thus, the warning is a canonical measure employed by the Ordinary to make persons aware of their obligation to properly regulate their conduct by doing some specific thing or omitting some specific thing in their manner of acting. While the warning is the mildest of the penal remedies,[48] the shades of intensity contained in the various definitions, indicates too that the warning may be given in a variety of degrees of calmness or forcefulness, depending upon the circumstances involved in any particular case.

SECTION A. THE USES OF THE WARNING

In pointing out the occasions when the warning may be employed, Vermeersch-Creusen,[49] Jone,[50] DeMeester,[51] Regatillo [52] and Cocchi [53] refer to the specifications contained in canon 2307. They state that warnings are to be used by the Ordinary upon someone who is either: 1) in the proximate occasion of committing a delict, or 2) revealed by the preliminary investigation to be under a grave suspicion of having already committed a delict. The scope of the warning is, therefore, always intimately connected with a delict.

In the first use of the warning considered by canon 2307, the offense in question has not yet been committed. If it does occur, however, the offense will fulfill the requirements of canon 2195 and be a true ecclesiastical delict. Here the law apparently attaches a punishment to the fact that a person places himself in the proximate occasion of committing a delict. The conduct of the person thus far has been at least exteriorly reprehensible [54] to the degree that he is considered to be in the proximate occasion [55] of com-

[48] Wernz, *Ius Decretalium*, VI, 259, n. 254.

[49] *Epitome*, III, 307, 502.

[50] *Commentarium*, III, 491.

[51] *Compendium*, p. 228, n. 1802.

[52] *Institutiones*, II, 532, n. 958.

[53] *Commentarium*, VIII, 208, n. 122.

[54] Ayrinhac-Lydon, *Penal Legislation*, p. 136, n. 180; Coronata, *Institutiones*, IV, 282, n. 1840.

[55] Blat notes that a proximate occasion is thus present whenever, by reason of repeated acts, an event follows most often from the nature of the circumstances involved, and results in an action or omission which is forbidden by a penal law or precept.—*Commentarium*, V, 189, n. 141.

mitting a delict, and he thereby makes himself liable to be given a warning about the matter. There has been some transgression, either by omission or positive action, which while not necessarily a delict itself, is intimately linked with a true delict and is the proximate occasion of its commission.[56]

It should not be overlooked here that the commission of one delict may also place a person in the proximate occasion of committing another delict and would thus be included in canon 2307. When the warning is issued in the above situations it is used as a preventive remedy seeking to impede an approaching evil by removing the voluntary occasions and proximate causes of delinquency.[57]

The second use of the warning involves the case where the preliminary inquiry has not produced sufficient proof to institute an accusatory action, but has left a grave suspicion that a crime was committed by a certain person.[58] The subject matter here may involve any type of delict which could be classified as such under either canon 2195 or canon 2222, § 1. The doubt which is involved may concern either the presence of the elements required for a delict, or the authorship of a delict which has certainly been committed. In order to employ the warning in such cases, the preliminary investigation must result in a suspicion of guilt which is well grounded,[59] being neither rash nor imprudent.[60] In speaking of such cases, Coronata remarks that certitude of the existence of the delict is not required here, but rather a suspicion which is not rash, but has some *fundamentum in re,* is sufficient grounds for using the warning.[61] This use of the warning prescribed by canon 2307 also has the characteristics of a preventive remedy, seeking to impede an approaching evil and to remove the stimuli of scandal.[62] In giving the warning on these occasions, the Ordinary is not

[56] Coronata, *Institutiones,* IV, 281, n. 1838; Cocchi, *Commentarium,* VIII, 207, n. 120.

[57] *Ad mentem Sacra Haec,* n. 2.

[58] Sipos, *Enchiridion,* p. 853; Berutti, *Institutiones,* VI, 240, n. 94; c. 1946, § 2, 2°.

[59] Ayrinhac-Lydon, *Penal Legislation,* p. 136, n. 180.

[60] Sipos, *Enchiridion,* p. 853.

[61] *Institutiones,* IV, 285, n. 1842.

[62] *Ad mentem Sacra Haec,* n. 2.

required to hear the defendant beforehand. Jone notes that the Ordinary should be urged to first hear the subject give an account or defense of his action, but no one is able to affirm that the Ordinary has violated a prescript of law if he does not listen to the suspect before he gives the warning.[63] Coronata substantiates this position when he states that an apportunity to offer a defense before being given a warning is not required by the Code in either canon 2307 or 1946, § 2, 2°, and that the matter is left entirely to the prudence of the Ordinary.[64]

The receiving of a warning is indeed in itself an opportunity to present the true facts of the case, and may thus serve as a great aid toward casting aside all suspicion and taint of guilt.[65]

The person who has been given a warning has the right to exonorate himself about the subject matter of the warning in order to exclude any imputability whatsoever. If he does successfully clear his name in the matter, the corrected person is able to require that no mention of the warning should be retained in the archives, or that along with the record of the warning the notation that he has completely cleared himself of all guilt or suspicion should be made also.[66]

The warning could also serve, of course, as the occasion for an admission of guilt and for a resolution of subsequent amendment of conduct.

Coronata points out that the two uses of the warning which are presented in canon 2307 do not constitute an exclusive list of all the occasions when the warning may be employed.[67] Although he does not specify what other uses could be added to the listing, this view is not without merit, and may be substantiated in the Code.

There are times when specifically determined punishments are prescribed by the law, and when these and only these may be imposed upon the delinquent. At other times, however, the law grants an option concerning which punishment is to be inflicted

[63] *Commentarium*, III, p. 491.

[64] *Institutiones*, IV, 285, n. 1842.

[65] Cf. Lega, *Praelectiones*, IV, 357, n. 287.

[66] Coronata, *Institutiones*, IV, 285, n. 1842.

[67] Cf. *Institutiones*, IV, 285, n. 1842.

and leaves the choice to the discretion of the Ordinary or judge. When the use of the penal remedies is prescribed, but no particular remedy is specified, such an option exists. In these latter cases, as long as the circumstances warrant its use, and there is reason to think that it will be effective, the warning may be employed.

Both canons 2223, § 3, 3° and 2224, § 2 permit the use of the penal remedies for cases involving delicts which are certain. Neither of these canons, however, indicates which of the penal remedies are to be used. Provided it would be otherwise apt to fulfill the purpose of employing the penal remedies in these cases, there is no reason to exclude the use of the warning here, even though it is the mildest of the remedies. The character of the delinquent, and other circumstances of the case would, of course, have much influence upon the decision to use the warning in any particular case.

Such a use of the warning, even for cases involving a delict which is certain, is at times in the best interest of equity, and would be in conformity with the gradual increase of severity which one finds in the list of the penal remedies in canon 2306.[68] Besides the uses of the warning indicated in canon 2307, therefore, it seems clear that this remedy may also be used in cases involving certain delicts, when it is prudently judged that such a measure will be efficacious and its use is not otherwise contrary to law.

SECTION B. CHARACTERISTICS OF THE WARNING

1. *Subject Matter of the Warning*

Usually the warning deals with duties of state in life or one or other obligation of proper conduct. The warning seeks to forestall scandals and delicts resulting from cases of imprudent and illicit friendships, intemperance in drink, the fostering of rash doctrine, forbidden business enterprises and speculation, visiting forbidden or dangerous places, subversion of authority, concubinage, a cleric neglecting to fulfill the divine offices correctly, a layman involved in marital infidelity or domestic irresponsibility, habits of vice, violence, dope-addiction and similar matters of

68 Roelker notes that apparently the remedies mentioned in canon 2306 are not to be used indiscriminately, but gradually, according to their need.—*Precepts*, p. 194.

conduct.[69] Any of the delicts which are specified by the Code, could, of course, be proper subject matter of a warning when the legal conditions for the use of the warning are present.

2. *Contents of the Warning*

a. The Notion of Blame is By-Passed

The warning is generally conceded to be of such a nature that it does not impute blame of delinquency to the person.[70] For many of the occasions when the warning is used, of course, the omission of reference to imputability for delinquency is imperative. One could hardly be blamed for a delict which he has not yet committed. It likewise seems equally unjust to attribute imputability to someone upon whom has fallen the grave suspicion of delinquency, but no actual sufficient proof of it exists. In the giving of a warning, therefore, the question of delictual blame or imputability is by-passed, and attention is rather given to the objective of making the person aware of what is to be done or omitted in the present dangerous situation.

b. Motivation in the Warning

In the warning the person is reminded of his obligations in the matter concerned, and it is brought to his attention what he should do or abstain from in order to avoid the evil of scandal or the delict which is impending. Lega suggests that an appeal may thus be made to a person's conscience, his usefulness, his good name.[71] Similar motives of the person's loyalty and love of God, the person's fine work in the past which is now in jeopardy, the consequences upon himself or upon others caused by his wayward conduct, may be used. Nor should the value of the fact that the Ordinary is trusting in the person's loyalty and cooperation be overlooked as a means of crime-preventive motivation. Besides giving attention to the particular obligation or duty which is concerned, therefore, the Ordinary may do well to fortify the warning with suitable motivation to secure its efficacy.

69 Lega, *Praelectiones*, IV, 356, n. 286.

70 DeMeester, *Compendium*, p. 228, n. 1803; Vermeersch-Creusen, *Epitome*, III, 307, n. 502.

71 *Praelectiones*, 354, n. 285.

c. Absence of the Threat of a Specific Penalty

While the warning involves something more than a general exhortation to virtue or friendly advice,[72] the motivation which the Ordinary may employ in issuing it should not include the threat of a penalty. The authors point out that this absence of a threatened penalty is a characteristic of the warning and a difference between the warning and the precept.[73] This trait, it may be recalled, also produced a basis of distinction between these two remedies in the pre-Code Instructions from the Holy See,[74] and in the legislation of the Third Plenary Council of Baltimore.[75]

d. The Warning Must be Made Specifically to the Person

The person who is being warned should be made aware that he is receiving a canonical warning. Hence it must be apparent to him that the warning is coming from competent authority and is being made specifically to him. This element of specific delivery to the person has been the traditional characteristic of canonical admonitions in the Church, and there is no indication that such requirement has ceased with the use of the penal remedies in the Code. As evidence of this tradition, one may look to a decretal of Pope Honorius III [1216-1227]. This decretal[76] discusses the case of a cleric who is a source of scandal because while receiving income from his benefice, he is also not only occupied in secular business but claims immunity from the local laws of commerce on the grounds of his clerical privilege. The Pope instructs the Bishop of Amiens to give the usual three admonitions to the cleric before the latter *ipso facto* loses his clerical privilege. In commenting on *tales tertio a te moniti* of this decretal, Panormitanus [† 1453] notes as the significant features of these admonitions: 1) they must come from the cleric's bishop; and 2) they must be made directly to the cleric, admonishing him to desist from the evil practice

72 Ayrinhac-Lydon, *Penal Legislation,* p. 136, n. 180.

73 Sipos, *Enchiridion,* p. 852; Jone, *Commentarium,* III, 491; Vermeersch-Creusen, *Epitome,* III, 307, n. 502.

74 Cf. Chapter I, p. 22.

75 Conc. Pl. Balt. III., n. 309—*Acta et Decreta,* p. 177: . . . sine ulla tamen comminatione poenae.

76 Honorius III to Everardus, Bishop of Amiens, 12 May 1218—Potthast, n. 5784; c. 16, X, *de vita et honestate clericorum,* III, 1.

which is the source of scandal.[77] Panormitanus further emphasizes the requirement of specific delivery of the admonition to the cleric himself by stating that a general warning that all the clergy must abstain from *negotiatio* would not be sufficient for the admonition in this case.[78]

It seems necessary to insist that this characteristic of particularity in administering ecclesiastical admonitions must be maintained and observed in the penal remedy of warning. Indeed, the warning must be made specifically to the person for whom it is intended, for one of the elements which makes canonical warnings to be punishments is the fact that they are addressed to the person individually.[79] The Ordinary must make sure that the warning is made directly to the person who is being warned, or else his efforts will not qualify as a canonical warning.

Because of this requirement of specific delivery of a warning, it is clear that a general warning to the clergy who are assembled at a clergy conference, retreat, or similar occasion, would not qualify as such a warning even though the Ordinary has a specific cleric in mind when he gives the general warning. The same may be said in regard to the laity if a general warning is given to the faithful in a pastoral letter, sermon, a parish meeting, or similar gatherings of the faithful. The penal remedy of warning must be addressed directly to the person whom it concerns.

e. The Ordinary is Indicated as the Author of the Warning

The Code makes it clear that the Ordinary is to be the author of the warning.[80] Since this authorship by the Ordinary gives the warning its canonical status,[81] it is the opinion of the present writer that if a third person is employed to give the warning, the person who is being warned must be informed that the warning comes from the Ordinary. Unless this authorship is made known to

[77] Abbas Panormitanus (Nicholas de Tudeschis), *Commentaria in Quinque Libros Decretalium* (5 vols. in 7, Venetiis, 1588), VI, 14, commentary on the decretal cited.

[78] *Loc. cit.*

[79] Cf. Smith, S. B., *Elements of Ecclesiastical Law*, III, 55, n. 1758.

[80] C. 2307: . . . Ordinarius per se vel per interpositam personam moneat.

[81] Cf. DeMeester, *Compendium*, p. 228, n. 1802; Berutti, *Institutiones*, VI, 240, n. 94; Lega, *Praelectiones*, IV, 353, n. 284.

the one who is given the warning, he may not be aware that he is receiving a canonical warning rather than a fraternal admonition; and hence he may not be aware of his greater obligation of co-operation and obedience. In order to make its canonical character manifest to the one being warned, the fact that the warning comes from the Ordinary must be made known to him. This requirement must be observed whether the warning is given personally by the Ordinary or by someone who is acting in his name.

3. *The Delivery of the Warning*

a. By the Ordinary Personally or Through an Intermediary

While the Ordinary must be the author of the warning, its actual delivery or manifestation to the person who is being warned may be made in several ways. It may be given personally by the Ordinary, or by a third party [82] who acts as his delegate. This arrangement for the delivery of the warning is a continuation of the pre-Code methods for imposing the canonical warnings of that legislation,[83] and the commentary previously made on this matter has equal application for this penal remedy of the Code.[84]

The choice of whether to proceed personally or through a third party is left to the discretion of the Ordinary. Undoubtedly the nature of the subject matter, the person involved, and the circumstances which are peculiar to a particular case will all have some influence on the decision of who will impose the warning. At times also the pressing demands of a heavy schedule will occasion the appointment of a third person by the Ordinary to act in his stead.

When the Ordinary chooses to have someone else impose the warning for him, he is employing the rule of law: *Potest quis per alium, quod potest facere per seipsum.*[85] Every intermediary should, of course, be chosen wisely and should be well suited for the task which he is required to perform. Lega points out that such a person should be conspicuous both for his prudence and his piety.[86]

[82] C. 2307.

[83] Cf. *Sacra Haec*, n. 6; *Cum Magnopere*, n. VI; Conc. Pl. Balt. III., n. 309.

[84] Cf. Chapter I, pp. 16, 17.

[85] Reg. 68, R. J. in VI°.

[86] *Praelectiones*, IV, 355, n. 285.

When the warning concerns a matter whose nature demands that it must remain secret, even greater care must be exercised in the choice of a suitable delegate.[87] Whenever it is thought advisable to use the services of a third person in giving a warning, Jone wisely suggests that the Vicar General, rural dean, or paster may be an apt choice for the task.[88]

b. By Letter

When canon 2307 is compared with the pre-Code law, one method of giving the warning seems to be missing in the present legislation. The Instructions of 1880 [89] and 1883 [90] as well as the *Decreta* of the Third Plenary Council of Baltimore.[91] All provided that the Ordinary could give a warning by letter. There is no such provision in canon 2307. However, one needs only to look to canon 2309, § 2 to find that the public warning may be given by letter.[92] To this consideration Blat adds that the secret warning may not only be given face to face, but also by letter.[93] Although not indicated in the Code, this manner of giving the secret warning by letter still applies in the United States of America by reason of the particular legislation for this country from the Third Plenary Council of Baltimore. Blat's position is well taken, therefore, at least for the application of the warning in this country.

Thus, the present legislation on the delivery of the warning is the same as the pre-Code law. The Ordinary may impose a warning personally, either face to face with the person being warned or by letter to him; or he may use the services of an intermediary third party.

4. *Modes for Issuing the Warning*

According to the Code of Canon Law there are two distinct modes which may be employed in the giving of a warning: 1)

[87] Vermeersch-Creusen, *Epitome,* III, 307, n. 503.

[88] *Commentarium,* III, 491.

[89] *Sacra Haec,* n. 6.

[90] *Cum Magnopere,* N. VI.

[91] Conc. Pl. Balt. III., n. 309—*Acta et Decreta,* p. 177.

[92] C. 2309, § 2: . . . vel per epistolam ita tamen ut de receptione et tenore epistolae ex aliquo documento constet.

[93] *Commentarium,* V, 191, n. 143.

secret and 2) public. By presenting these modes in such terminology, the present legislation has done much to clarify their concepts.

It is interesting to note here that in the preliminary schema of the present Code, the canon which is now canon 2309, § 1 was worded as follows: *Tam correptio quam monitio potest esse vel paterna seu secreta, vel publica.*[94] In the promulgated edition of the Code, however, the word *paterna* was eliminated, and grounds for misunderstanding were likewise thereby eliminated.[95] It seems to the present writer that this deletion is significant not of the fact that the warning cannot now be given in a paternal manner by the Ordinary, but rather that the paternal aspect (which may, but need not be present in the warning) should not be emphasized to the extent that the canonical nature of the warning is overlooked. The use of *paterna* could lead someone to think of the secret warning solely as a charitable admonition, and overlook the fact that it is a canonical jurisdictional measure requiring the same response of obedience as the public warning. This possible confusion of concepts is eliminated by the present wording of canon 2309, § 1. In speaking of the secret warning, Vermeersch-Creusen point out that the Code does not forbid the Ordinaries to proceed paternally if this method of approach is able efficaciously to remove the defendant from his evil way of acting. They aptly state, however, that a distinction must be made between a paternal admonition and a canonical warning which is given in a paternal manner,[96] and that the penal remedy of warning does not concern the paternal admonition.

At present, most authors[97] adhere to a relatively consistent terminology in regard to the warning and the rebuke. In accord with the distinction made in the Code, they divide both warnings and rebukes into the categories of public and secret. The specific difference between these two modes rests fundamentally on the basis

[94] Cf. Gasparri, *Schema Codicis Iuris Canonici* (4 vols. in 2, Romae, 1913), IV, 54, c. 112, § 2.

[95] The presentation of the modes in the Code by canon 2309, § 1 reads: Tam monitio quam correptio potest esse vel publica vel secreta.

[96] *Epitome,* III, 308, n. 503.

[97] E. g., Vermeersch-Creusen, DeMeester, Regatillo, Coronata, et al.

that, while the effect produced by both is canonical, they differ in regard to the presence (or absence) of legal formalities when they are given.[98]

a. The Public Warning

A warning is called public if it is given either before a notary or two witnesses or else by letter, but in such a manner that the receipt and contents of the letter can be established by some document.[99] By these various methods the warning becomes public in so far as it is known to the law to be such.[100] The name public does not, however, imply that the fact and circumstances involved in the warning are necessarily now the possession and subject of public knowledge and general conversation. While the warning may be juridically public, the Ordinary is still able to require an oath of secrecy from the notary or witnesses before whom the public warning is given.[101]

The Code lists the three ways of giving a canonical public warning, and it is left to the Ordinary or his delegate to choose which method is to be used for any particular case.[102]

1. The first method of giving a public warning requires the presence of the chancellor[103] or other notary of the curia[104] when the warning is being given. In such circumstances, the warning may be given orally.[105] While it adds solemnity to the occasion and is somewhat of an advantage for the Ordinary to have a prepared text of the warning which he may read to the person being warned, there seems to be no requirement of this feature by the law.

2. The second method of giving a public warning requires the presence of two witnesses. In selecting persons to act as witnesses of a public warning, the qualifications required for witnesses to be

98 DeMeester, *Compendium*, p. 229, n. 1804; Regatillo, *Institutiones* II, 532, n. 959; Coronata, *Institutiones*, IV, 284, n. 1841.

99 C. 2309, § 2.

100 Cf. Messmer, *Canonical Procedure*, p. 151.

101 Berutti, *Institutiones*, VI, 241, n. 96.

102 Coronata, *Institutiones*, IV, 283, n. 1841; Berutti, *Institutiones*, VI, 241, n. 96.

103 C. 372, § 3.

104 C. 1585.

105 Sipos, *Enchiridion*, p. 853.

acceptable to give judicial testimony according to canons 1756-1757 should be kept in mind. In the event that the matter must proceed to formal trial, the testimony of the witnesses that the warning was given will be important. Since the law itself would hardly prescribe witnesses whom it finds objectionable, the requirement which the Code seems to demand here for a public warning is the presence of two persons who are capable of experiencing and understanding the fact that a warning is being given, and who are also *omni exceptioni maiores.*

In both of the methods mentioned above, it is the presence of the notary or the two witnesses which makes the warning public.

The Code requires that a record must be kept to the effect that a warning was given to the person.[106] In the case of a public warning, it seems that its public character should be noted in this record together with an identification of the notary or the witnesses who were present. The record should furthermore be made an authentic document by affixing the signature either of the Ordinary who issued the warning or of a notary.[107] It should be recalled here that while the signature of the notary or other public person is always essential for the validity of a public document,[108] the use of a seal or other formalties might also be required by custom or particular law. While it is also a general and useful practice to indicate the date and place on the document, according to a decision of the Rota on December 6, 1909, a document is not invalid if this information is omitted.[109] It is well, however, that this information should be included. Furthermore, although the *acta* or record of the preliminary investigation of the case contains an indication of the subject matter which is involved, it is desirable to have this also included in the record of the warning.

3. Besides the presence of a notary or two witnesses, a public warning may also be given by letter. In this third method it is required that the Ordinary retains a document which establishes

[106] C. 2309, § 5.

[107] C. 1813, § 1, 1°-2°; Sipos, *Enchiridion*, p. 853; Jone, *Commentarium*, III, 174.

[108] Cf. c. 1813, § 1, 1°; Coronata, *Institutiones*, III, 286, n. 1341.

[109] Jone, *Commentarium*, III, 174.

full faith and credit [110] for the receipt and the contents of the letter [111] in which the warning is given.

Normally such a letter will be written on official stationery and contain an indication of: the date and place it is written, the name and address of the person to whom it is written, the fact that a warning is being given, the subject matter of the warning, and will be signed by the Ordinary. The use of the seal of the Ordinary might also be customary.

The letter may be sent by public registered mail requesting a signed receipt, or by curial messenger.[112] The reception of the letter is verified by a signed receipt or by the documentary testimony of the messenger who delivered it.[113] The purpose of this receipt is to furnish proof or to give faith to the fact that the warning was given and received.[114]

In the event that the letter is refused, this will be noted also and the letter returned to the Ordinary. Coronata notes that whoever refuses to accept a letter, or in some manner impedes its delivery is considered to have received it.[115] Such a refusal would be significant of the fact that more severe measures are needed in this particular case.

The contents of the letter are verified by having an authentic copy of the entire letter made and preserved in the *acta* of the case.[116] The copy is authenticated by the signature either of the Ordinary or a notary.[117]

Coronata states that the authentic copy of the public warning should be preserved in the public archives of the curia. He hastens to add, however, that this does not mean that the contents of the letter would be available and could be shown to everyone indis-

[110] Cf. c. 1813, § 1, 1°; c. 1816.

[111] C. 2309, § 2.

[112] Sipos, *Enchiridion*, p. 853; Ayrinhac-Lydon, *Penal Legislation*, p. 137, n. 181; c. 2143, § 1; c. 1719.

[113] Blat, *Commentarium*, V, 191, n. 143.

[114] Cf. Berutti, *Institutiones*, VI, 241, n. 96.

[115] *Institutiones*, IV, 283, n. 1841; cf. cc. 2143, 1718, 1719.

[116] Jone, *Commentarium*, III, 492; Coronata, *Institutiones*, IV, 283, n. 1841.

[117] C. 1813, § 1, 1°.

criminately.[118] It is his position that one of the characteristic differences between the public warning and the secret warning is that, while a copy of the former should be preserved in its entirety in the non-secret archives, the document referring to the latter need not be a copy of the entire letter and should be kept in the secret archives.[119]

That it is possible to protect a person's good name, even though his record is kept in the public archives of the curia, no one can deny. Indeed, the proper care and control of the public records in both parochial and diocesan archives in this regard is part of a marvelous tradition of the Church in the United States. In the matter of warnings and rebukes, however, it seems that the Church wishes the maximum of caution to be exercised over the records or memoranda of their issuance. Canon 2309, § 5 provides that a warning or rebuke, even though given secretly, must be verified by some document which is preserved in the secret archives.[120] From its wording, this canon apparently presumes that the records of public warning and rebuke are to be kept in the secret archives, and indicates that a record of the secret warning and rebuke is to be made and kept in the secret archives as well.

On the basis of canon 2309, § 5, the present writer holds that a record of every penal remedy of warning and rebuke must be kept in the secret archives. Berutti is substantially in accord with this opinion. He states that the authentic copy of the public warning given by letter should be kept in the secret archives of the curia, and he reasons that documents which are relative to criminal matters are usually kept in the secret archives because this procedure is clearly in conformity with the prescriptions of canon 379, § 1.[121]

While Jone does not mention the possibility that all records of both public and secret warnings should be kept in the secret archives, he does note that although a document may deal with a

118 *Institutiones*, IV, 283, n. 1841.

119 *Institutiones*, IV, 284, n. 1841.

120 C. 2309, § 5: De monitione et correptione, etsi secreto factae fuerint, constare debet ex aliquo documento in secreto archivo Curiae asservando.

121 *Institutiones*, VI, 241, n. 96.

matter which is *de jure* public, it may happen that this should be kept in the secret archives.[122]

b. The Secret Warning

The other mode by which the Ordinary may issue a warning is the secret warning. This type is given in the absence of those legal formalities which are prescribed for the public warning by canon 2309, § 2. Thus, this warning is issued without the presence of a notary or witnesses,[123] and it may also be given by letter,[124] without observing all of the formalities regarding retaining documentary evidence for the receipt and the contents of the warning.

The subject matter which occasions the use of the secret warning may be the same as that for which the public warning is given. The Code does not determine whether the secret or the public warning should be used in a particular case, but apparently this is left to the prudent judgment of the Ordinary.[125] Cocchi maintains that the decision of which mode of the warning is employed should be based to a great extent upon the judgment of which one will be the more efficacious.[126] Since, however, there is apparently a lesser punishment involved in receiving a secret warning,[127] it seems to the present writer that this mode of the warning should be employed first as long as the Ordinary judges that there is reasonable hope that its use will be efficacious. Furthermore, at times the nature of the subject matter itself requires that a secret warning should be given. As Coronata remarks, if the suspicion of delictual conduct is not generally known, or the matter is considered to be occult, then the secret warning should be given.[128]

While the secret warning is issued without the formalities which are associated with the public warning, the Code does require that its existence should be verified by some document which is kept

[122] *Commentarium,* III, 492.

[123] Cocchi, *Commentarium,* VIII, 208, n. 122.

[124] Sipos, *Enchiridion,* p. 853.

[125] Cf. Coronata, *Institutiones,* IV, 285, n. 1841.

[126] *Commentarium,* VIII, 208, n. 122.

[127] Cf. Lega, *Praelectiones,* IV, 349, n. 278; Berutti, *Institutiones,* VI, 241, n. 96.

[128] *Institutiones,* IV, 285, n. 1842; also Ayrinhac-Lydon, *Penal Legislation,* p. 127, n. 181.

in the secret archives of the curia.[129] Apparently such a document would exist if only a memorandum were made by the Ordinary to the effect that the warning had been given by him to the person involved, together with an indication of the subject matter of the warning. No copy of the warning itself need be made or retained. As was previously noted, Coronata points out that one of the differences between the public and the secret warning is that the existence of the public warning must be verified with an authentic copy of the whole text of the warning.[130]

Because of the absence of witnesses when the secret warning is given, the memorandum of it, together with a record of the preliminary investigation of the matter which occasioned it, are very important. These records will prove to be very useful toward verifying the propriety of the Ordinary's action in the event that the person who is corrected seeks legimate recourse from higher authority.[131]

There is no doubt concerning where the document relative to the giving of a secret warning must be preserved. The Code specifies that it must be kept in the secret archives.[132] This provision of the Code is in accord with the previous directive of the Sacred Congregation for Bishops and Regulars of September 7, 1801 which forbade such notations to be kept in the public archives.[133]

5. *Repetition of the Warning*

The nature of the warning allows for its repetition if there is hope that such action will efficaciously recall the person to better conduct.[134] While the warning may be given to the same person in regard to several subsequent and different matters, it may also be given more than once even in the same case.[135]

129 Cf. c. 2309, § 5.

130 *Institutiones*, IV, 284, n. 1841.

131 As a remedy of law, recourse to higher authority is available to someone who maintains that the penal remedies have been unjustly inflicted upon him—Cf. Jone, *Commentarium*, III, p. 493; Coronata, *Institutiones*, IV, 285, n. 1842. DeMeester notes that such recourse is *in devolutivo*—*Compendium*, p. 231, n. 1807.

132 C. 2309, § 5.

133 Cf. *Analecta Iuris Pontificium*, XX (1881), p. 82.

134 Berutti, *Institutiones*, VI, 242, n. 96.

135 Blat, *Commentarium*, V, 191, n. 143.

In any particular case, the use or the repetition of the warning is left to the judgment of the Ordinary or judge and his prudent evaluation of the circumstances involved.[136] Thus, for proper reasons, the warning may be repeated several times before the Ordinary may feel obliged to resort to more severe measures.

If, on the other hand, the Ordinary considers that the use of the warning will be fruitless, he may omit it altogether and employ the precept instead.[137]

Whenever the warning is repeated, Coronata wisely points out that this fact should be recorded on the memorandum of the general contents or copy of the warning which is preserved in the archives.[138]

ARTICLE IV. THE REBUKE (*Correptio*)

The rebuke is typified as an upbraiding,[139] a strong blaming or scolding,[140] or a vigorous reproach[141] given by an Ordinary to someone who has been convicted of or confessed to a delict or whose frequent way of acting has given rise to scandal or a grave disturbance of order.[142] This penal remedy differs from the warning because it adds the element of reproach or blame to the warning,[143] and is normally employed against a graver disturbance of order.[144] In giving the rebuke, it is the culpability of the person's way of acting which is vigorously reproached as the cause

136 C. 2309, § 6: . . . monitio fieri potest semel vel pluries, pro Superioris arbitrio et prudentia. As was seen previously, the term *Superior* is understood here to be used as a synonym for the Ordinary and the judge.—Cf. Chapter II, p. 61.

137 C. 2310.

138 *Institutiones*, IV, 285, n. 1842.

139 Vermeersch-Creusen, *Epitome*, III, 307, n. 502; Cocchi, *Commentarium*, VIII, 209, n. 123.

140 Sipos, *Enchiridion*, p. 853; Coronata, *Institutiones*, IV, 286, n. 1843; Regatillo, *Institutiones*, II, 532, n. 959.

141 Jone, *Commentarium*, III, 491.

142 Cc. 2308; 2309, § 3.

143 Cf. DeMeester, *Compendium*, p. 228, n. 1803; Vermeersch-Creusen, *Epitome*, III, 307, n. 502 .

144 Coronata, *Institutiones*, IV, 286, n. 1843.

of scandal or a grave disturbance of order.[145] The rebuke, therefore, emphasizes the element of responsibility for the delict or grave conduct.

Lest the rebuke may be completely useless, it is imperative that what is being corrected is clearly indicated. This clear definition of the subject matter of the rebuke eliminates any basis for misunderstanding about what is involved, and presents a suitable opportunity for the corrected person to offer his defense, if he so desires. Very appropriately does Berutti remark that the subject matter of the rebuke must be sharply specified, or else the correction and reformation of the person will not be promoted, but only exasperation will be enkindled.[146]

The subject matter which is an occasion for giving a rebuke may be the commission of a true delict,[147] or it may involve a frequent manner of acting which is sufficiently grave that an evil custom has begun even though a true delict need not be present.[148] There is no question of mere suspicion here. When there is not a certain delict present, there must be conduct which certainly results in scandal (i. e., the commission of a grave sin by another), or a grave disturbance of a parish, diocese, or similar territory.[149] As possible occasions for the use of the rebuke, Ayrinhac-Lydon cite such examples as imprudent sermons and dangerous companionships.[150]

Since canon 2308 refers to someone's frequent way of acting,[151] it seems reasonable to conclude that a single act or a few infrequent acts would not be sufficient to require the use of the rebuke unless such acts were true delicts. It must be recalled here, however, that the Ordinary is able to inflict a punishment whenever scandal is produced or a transgression of special gravity is committed, even

145 Jone, *Commentarium*, III, 491.

146 *Institutiones*, VI, 242, n. 96.

147 Cf. Coronata, *Institutiones*, IV, 286, n. 1843; Regatillo, *Institutiones*, II, 532, n. 959.

148 Jone, *Commentarium*, III, 491; Vermeersch-Creusen, *Epitome*, III, 307, n. 502; Blat, *Commentarium*, V, 190, n. 142; Sipos, *Enchiridion*, p. 853.

149 Cf. Blat, *Commentarium*, V, 190, n. 142.

150 *Penal Legislation*, p. 136, n. 180.

151 C. 2308: . . . ex alicuius conversatione . . .

though no specific penal law has been broken.[152] What action, if any, is taken in any such particular case is left to the prudent discretion of the Ordinary.

SECTION A. JURIDIC SIMILARITIES SHARED BY WARNING AND REBUKE

While being distinct from the penal remedy of warning, much of what has been said of the warning applies equally to the rebuke. Thus, the Code provides that: 1) the rebuke, too, may be public or secret[153] (the public rebuke being given before a notary or two witnesses or by letter in such a manner that the receipt and contents of the letter are verified by some document;[154] the secret rebuke being given by spoken word or in writing with an absence of the legal formalities for the public rebuke).[155] 2) A copy or memorandum of the general contents of all rebukes must be preserved in the secret archives of the curia[156] in case the matter goes to further process, or for the protection and defense of the Ordinary's action.[157] In this document, there should be indicated to whom, for what reason, by whom, and when the rebuke is given. For a public rebuke by letter, the copy of the whole letter must be preserved.[158] 3) The rebuke may be given once or several times according to the judgment and prudence of the Ordinary.[159] 4) When the legal conditions are present, the rebuke may be by-passed and the precept employed immediately by the Ordinary.[160] 5) The rebuke may be given by the Ordinary personally or through an intermediary or else by letter.[161] The choice of which of these procedures is to be followed is left to the prudent judgment of the Ordinary. The motivation for the choice of one method in

[152] Cf. c. 2222, § 1.

[153] C. 2309, § 1.

[154] C. 2309, § 2; c. 1722.

[155] Berutti, *Institutiones*, VI, 242, n. 96.

[156] C. 2309, § 5.

[157] Vermeersch-Creusen, *Epitome*, III, 308, n. 503.

[158] Berutti, *Institutiones*, VI, 242, n. 96; c. 2309, § 5, § 2.

[159] C. 2309, § 6.

[160] C. 2310.

[161] C. 2308.

preference to another follows the same pattern as was presented in the discussion of the warning [162] and the pre-Code legislation.[163]

SECTION B. REBUKE ACCOMMODATED TO THE CONDITIONS OF PERSON AND FACTS OF THE CASE

The rebuke may be given not only in various modes and methods of delivery, but also with various degrees of reproach and reprimand. For this reason the Code specifies that the rebuke should be accomodated to the particular conditions of the person as well as the nature of the facts of the case.[164] In this provision of canon 2308, a two-fold principle or guide for the application of the rebuke is outlined. Due consideration must be given by the Ordinary both to the 1) condition of the person and 2) the particular facts of the case. By this principle the Church points to the equity and spirit of fairness which must accompany the use of the penal remedies. While being firmly directed toward their preventive-repressive goal, the penal remedies must always be used in such a manner that the good name, feelings, and reputation of the persons involved will be safeguarded as much as possible.[165] Indeed, the dignity and propriety which are in keeping with the person and office of the Ordinary, as well as the personal integrity of the person being corrected, must be given due consideration when the manner of inflicting punishments is in question. The objective of the Church is to prescribe punishments which are humane and yet adequate to maintain Her social order.

In regard to the condition of the person, which must receive due attention in the giving of a rebuke, such factors as age, mental and physical health, position or state in life, type of personality, titles of honor, etc. must receive consideration.[166] Thus, while fulfilling his obligation of giving the rebuke, the Ordinary will resort to different degrees of vigor and methods of reproach when

[162] Cf. Chapter IV, p. 121.

[163] Cf. Chapter I, p. 16.

[164] C. 2308: . . . peculiaribus accommodatae conditionibus personae et facti de quo agitur.

[165] Cf. Ayrinhac-Lydon, *Penal Legislation*, p. 136.

[166] Cf. Ayrinhac-Lydon, *Penal Legislation*, p. 137; Cocchi, *Commentarium*, VIII, 209, n. 123; Blat, *Commentarium*, V, 190, n. 142.

dealing with the laity or the clergy, the foolishness of the imprudent youth, the aberrations of the mature adult, the follies of the senile. Those in good health may be rebuked in one manner, while another and more gentle reproach may seem apt for those weakened by sickness or suffering from some types of mental or psychic difficulties.

Along with the condition of the person, the facts of a particular case will also have bearing upon the manner in which a rebuke is given. The seriousness of the subject matter, of course, demands attention in this regard. Moreover, the circumstances attached to the subject matter must likewise be considered. Thus, those faults which result from imprudence or spontaneity of action may receive one treatment, while those which are the consequences of a depraved and malicious will require a different rebuke.[167] Furthermore, the past record of the person in its relation to the facts of the present case should be considered,[168] e. g. the first-offender may be punished in different fashion from someone who has received repeated warnings for repeated offenses.[169] Indeed, it would seem that most often the rebuke given to persons in these two classifications will differ greatly both in content and intensity of force with which thy are given. In each case great tact and wisdom are needed in order to effectively prevent the repetition of delicts, and yet all the while assist a person in his need to maintain his personal integrity and spiritual interest in life and his life's work.

The widespread nature of the scandal or the greatness of the disturbance of order merits attention also. The same may be said about the type of evidence, whether *prima facie* or only circumstantial, and the degree of proof which it had concerning the occasion for giving the rebuke. All of these elements may play a part in the deliberation which is left to the prudent consideration of the Ordinary and his consequent choice of words and manner of giving the rebuke in a particular case.

SECTION C. THE PUBLIC REBUKE

Besides the many similarities which it shares with the warning,

[167] Vermeersch-Creusen, *Epitome,* III, 308, n. 503.

[168] Ayrinhac-Lydon, *Penal Legislation,* p. 137.

[169] Cocchi, *Commentarium,* VIII, 209, n. 123.

there are several features of the rebuke which require attention in order to complement the consideration of this penal remedy.

While the same division between public and secret as exists for the warning is applied also to the rebuke, the Code requires that the public rebuke may be used only against a defendant who either has been convicted of a delict or has confessed to it.[170] Of course, such matters need not always necessitate a public rebuke. The rebuke may be given in either of two modes, public or secret.[171] If, however, the public rebuke is employed, the person being corrected must either have been convicted of or confessed to the commission of a delict. This characteristic is understandable when one adverts to the view of Ayrinhac-Lydon that the public rebuke may be very humiliating to the person upon whom it is imposed.[172] The certainty which is required, thus assures that no injustice will be imprudently or hastily inflicted upon the delinquent.

1. *Species of Public Rebuke*

Public rebuke is itself divided into species: 1) judicial and 2) extra judicial.[173]

a. The Judicial Public Rebuke

The term *judicial* as employed in relation to the rebuke refers not only to that which is given by a competent ecclesiastical judge presiding in court, but also to the rebuke given legimately by the Ordinary before a criminal trial begins.[174]

(1) Given by the Judge

Before the trial has begun, the judge has no power to inflict a punishment [175] nor is it his prerogative to decide whether a judicial rebuke may precede a criminal trial. His jurisdiction in regard to the rebuke is always limited to the extent that its exercise is restricted within the framework of the judicial process. For the

170 C. 2309, § 3; Cocchi, *Commentarium,* VIII, 209, n. 123.

171 Cf. c. 2309, § 1.

172 *Penal Legislation,* p. 136, n. 180.

173 *Ad mentem* c. 2309, § 3.

174 Cf. c. 2309, § 3; Ayrinhac-Lydon, *Penal Legislation,* p. 137, n. 181; Coronata, *Institutiones,* IV, 286, n. 1844.

175 Vermeersch-Creusen, *Epitome,* III, 139, n. 267.

judicial rebuke to be given by a judge, the safeguards and norms of formal procedure contained in Book IV of the Code must be followed. The judge must be presiding over his tribunal.[176]

(2) Given by the Ordinary

The judicial rebuke given by the Ordinary has a different aspect from that which is issued by the judge. The Ordinary may properly impose a judicial rebuke prior to the actual criminal trial.[177] Such a rebuke would seem to be aptly termed as extra-judicial, but the Code specifies that this, too, is a judicial rebuke. On this point, Vermeersch-Creusen state that this rebuke is called judicial because of the intimate connection which it has with a trial.[178]

The public judicial rebuke may be given by the Ordinary before a trial only when the delinquent has confessed to his crime. Besides this confession of guilt, the provisions of the Code concerning the proper use of the judicial rebuke must be kept in mind.[179]

The subject matter for the judicial rebuke by the Ordinary consists in delicts already committed which are *per se* material for judicial action.[180] There are, however, some delicts which because of their gravity, nature, or circumstances, do not admit the legimate use of the rebuke in such a manner. The Code thus excludes the use of the judicial rebuke by the Ordinary in the following cases:

1. When delicts involve excommunication either most especially or especially reserved to the Apostolic See, or privation of a benefice, infamy, deposition, or degradation.[181]

2. When someone has already incurred a *latae sententiae* vindictive penalty or a censure, and it is a matter now of merely issuing a declaratory sentence.[182]

3. When the Ordinary judges that the rebuke is not a sufficient means in a particular case to repair the scandal and restore the harm against justice which have resulted from the delict.[183]

[176] C. 2309, § 3: . . . si fiat a judice pro tribunali sedente. . . .

[177] C. 2309, § 3: . . . ab Ordinario ante processum criminalem. . . .

[178] *Epitome*, III, 139, n. 267.

[179] Cf. c. 1947; 953.

[180] Vermeersch-Creusen, *Epitome*, III, 139, n. 267.

[181] C. 1948, 1°.

[182] C. 1948, 2°.

[183] C. 1948, 3°.

4. When the delinquent has already been given two judicial rebukes, he is no longer eligible for a third rebuke. The matter must proceed to a formal criminal trial.[184]

In all other cases, if the cited defendant, upon being interrogated, confesses to the delict, the Ordinary should impose a rebuke instead of taking the matter further to criminal trial. The rebuke is thus used in place of a penalty,[185] especially when the delict does not involve a *recidivus.*[186]

The proper use of the judicial rebuke by the Ordinary before a criminal process requires that the defendant must be interrogated.[187] This interrogation may follow the same general pattern as that which is used in regard to a witness, except that the defendant is not required to take an oath to speak the truth.[188] The purpose of this interrogation is, of course, to obtain the defendant's confession of guilt. Toward the end of achieving this confession it would seem legitimate to make known to him the proofs of the delict which have been acquired in the preliminary investigation of the matter. The fact that the rebuke, rather than a criminal trial and its more servere subsequent penalty, may result from a confession of guilt, could also be used to motivate a confession. Even when the delict is notorious, Jone notes that there must still be an interrogation of the defendant in order to fulfill the requirement that a rebuke may be given after the delinquent has confessed to the commission of the delict.[189]

Consequent to the confession of the delinquent, the Ordinary is obliged to use the rebuke instead of having the matter proceed to criminal trial as long as such action is considered adequate to preserve the social order of the Church,[190] and would not be foreseen to be useless.[191]

The rebuke may be given at the same time that the defendant

[184] C. 1949, §§ 1, 2.

[185] *Ad mentem* c. 2309, § 4.

[186] Cocchi, *Commentarium*, VIII, 209, n. 123.

[187] C. 1947: Si reus interrogatus. . . .

[188] Cf. c. 1744.

[189] *Commentarium*, III, 269.

[190] *Ad mentem* C. 1948, 3°.

[191] Cf. c. 2310.

confesses to the delict, or else it may be issued at a subsequent meeting. Whenever it is given, Jone points out that a characteristic of this judicial rebuke demands that it must be given in the presence of a notary, since it is judicial.[192]

Canon 2309, § 3 refers to the penal remedy of the judicial rebuke as being given by the Ordinary prior to a criminal process.[193] However, canon 1950 also provides for the rebuke to be given by the Ordinary even after the trial has begun, and allows its use until the time before the conclusion of the cause.[194] The authors note that the judicial rebuke may thus be either used before or after the *litis contestatio* even until the closing of the cause, but not after the closing of the case.[195]

At times, a judicial rebuke is given by the judge or the Ordinary to increase a penalty, especially if a *recidivus* is involved.[196] The rebuke is thus intended as a preventive of future crime by giving greater efficacy to the penalty, and as more surely securing an efficacious purpose of amendment from the delinquent.[197]

The use of the judicial rebuke, the Code also indicates, may frequently be accompanied by other opportune remedies, penances, pious works, etc., which are intended as apt means of public reparation of scandal and the breach of justice.[198] Vermeersch-Creusen observe that such measures as a public apology and public retraction may be included among these remedies.[199] Such remedies would not, of course, be penal remedies, but would rather be vindictive measures which accompany the giving of a rebuke. These salutary remedies, pious works, and penances which are prescribed for the delinquent should be less severe in nature than the penalty which would have resulted from conviction by a criminal process.[200]

[192] *Commentarium,* III, 269.

[193] C. 2309, § 3: . . . vel ab Ordinario ante processum criminalem.

[194] C. 1950: . . . potest correptio ab Ordinario adhiberi non solum antequam gradus fiat ad formale iudicium, sed etiam eo incepto ante conclusionem in causa; . . . .

[195] E. g. Vermeersch-Creusen, *Epitome,* III, 140, n. 269; Berutti, *Institutiones,* VI, 242, n. 96.

[196] Cf. c. 2309, § 4; c. 1952; c. 2234; c. 2224, § 2.

[197] Cf. Ayrinhac-Lydon, *Penal Legislation,* p. 137, n. 181.

[198] Cf. c. 1952; Coronata, *Institutiones,* IV, 286, n. 1843.

[199] *Epitome,* III, 140, n. 270.

[200] Cf. c. 1952, § 2.

b. Extra-Judicial Public Rebuke

When not connected with a trial, the public rebuke may be given extra-judicially in any of the methods listed in canon 2309, § 2. This action would, of course, be subsequent to the requisite of a confession of guilt by the delinquent.

Even after a delinquent has been judicially convicted of guilt, the Ordinary may choose to issue the rebuke in the presence of two witnesses [201] or by letter. In such cases the rebuke would be public in accord with canon 2309, § 2, but would be extra-judicial.

SECTION D. THE SECRET REBUKE

The secret rebuke (that which lacks the formalities prescribed for a public rebuke)[202] is administered extra-judicially. Coronata states that the extra-judicial rebuke is given outside the circumstances of a criminal trial, with the Ordinary proceeding extra-judicially to secure for himself the proofs of the delict or scandal.[203] It seems that the secret rebuke could be used when either the delinquent has confessed or has been convicted, but would be especially useful when these conditions are absent and yet the Ordinary has sufficient indications of guilt that he is justified in issuing a rebuke.

Both Coronata and Jone note that, while the Ordinary proceeds extra-judicially, he must exercise care to collect his proofs, so that he will be able to defend the prudence of his action, in case the rebuked person seeks recourse from a competent higher authority.[204]

At times, some punishment or pious work which seems suitable to the particular case may accompany an extra-judicial rebuke.[205]

Contingent upon the good judgment of the Ordinary, the extra-judicial rebuke may be given once or several times.[206] There is no reason to believe that its use or repetition is limited as the judicial

201 Cf. Jone, *Commentarium*, III, 269.

202 Cf. c. 2309, §§ 1, 2.

203 *Institutiones*, IV, 287, n. 1845.

204 Jone, *Commentarium*, III, 492; Coronata, *Institutiones*, IV, 287, n. 1845.

205 Cf. Coronata, *Institutiones*, IV, 287, n. 1845.

206 C. 2309, § 6.

rebuke is, the latter being restricted to be used not more than twice upon the same defendant for the same crime.

ARTICLE V. THE PRECEPT (*Praceptum*)

The penal remedy of precept is a command or order given by a competent ecclesiastical authority, in which an accurate indication of what is to be done or what is to be avoided is joined with a threat of a penalty in case of transgression.[207]

Roelker [208] notes that in Canon Law the term *precept* can be used in reference to three different entities: 1) A command to do or avoid something, without any reference to a penalty; 2) A command to do or avoid something, together with the threat of a penalty; and 3) The command to endure the actual infliction of a penalty. The precept as a penal remedy is contained in the second of these classifications. Every particular penal precept is, of course, not a penal remedy, for such precepts may be issued for reasons other than the crime-prevention objective of the remedies. The penal remedy of precept is, however, one type of particular penal precept.[209]

SECTION A. THE ESSENTIAL ELEMENTS OF THE PRECEPT

The precept differs from the warning and the rebuke in so far as it is a graver remedy, testing the contumacy of the delinquent [210] and containing the explicit threat of a penalty.[211]

Considered in itself, the precept contains three essential elements:

1. A command given by a competent ecclesiastical authority.
2. An accurate indication of what is to be done or avoided by the person who is given the command.

[207] Cf. c. 2310; Coronata, *Institutiones*, IV, 287, n. 1846; Sipos, *Enchiridion*, p. 853; Regatillo, *Institutiones*, II, 532, n. 960; Cocchi, *Commentarium*, VIII, 210, n. 124.

[208] *Precepts*, p. 166.

[209] Cf. Berutti, *Institutiones*, VI, 242, n. 97; Coronata, *Institutiones*, IV, 288, n. 1846. Since this is the only type of precept which is the subject of this section, hereafter it will simply be referred to as precept.

[210] Cocchi, *Commentarium*, VIII, 210, n. 124.

[211] Ayrinhac-Lydon, *Penal Legislation*, p. 138, n. 182.

3. A clear threat of a penalty to which the person will be subject in case he transgresses the command.

Whenever a precept is given, it must be done in such a manner that these constitutive elements are evident to the person being corrcted.

1. *A Commnad Given by a Competent Ecclesiastical Authority*

In order that a precept exist, an actual command or order must be given. Although the Ordinary may have resorted to suggesting, urging, and counseling, until he has issued a command, the precept does not exist.[212] It is the command then, which significantly indicates that a precept is being given. In regard to this feature, Roelker wisely observes that it is necessary that the command of the Ordinary be understood as such, and not as a suggesting of counsel or as a mere recommendation of a mode of action.[213]

Beyond any notion of exhortation, the command in a precept particularizes and personally emphasizes the obedience which is due because of the juridic relationship which exists between the Ordinary and the person being corrected.[214] The precept, thus based upon the individual relationship between the Ordinary and the person being corrected, produces an entirely personal obligation of obedience.[215] This obedience is a matter of conscience for the person who is given the precept.[216]

2. *An Accurate Indication of What is to be Done or Avoided by the Person Who is Given the Command*

Every command must have a subject matter, i. e., it must command something. The subject matter of the precept is an accurate indication of what is to be done or what should be avoided by the person who is given the command.[217]

212 Cf. Roelker, *Precepts*, p. 3.

213 *Precepts*, p. 6.

214 Cf. Roelker, *Precepts*, p. 105; p. 3.

215 Cf. Roelker, *Precepts*, p. 106.

216 Blat, *Commentarium*, V, 180, n. 140.

217 C. 2310: . . . datur praeceptum, quo quid agere quidve evitare praeventus debeat, accurate indicetur, . . . ; Coronata, *Institutiones*, IV, 287, n. 1846; *Regatillo, Institutiones*, II, 532, n. 960; Cocchi, *Commentarium*, VIII, 210, n. 124.

According to the nature of its subject matter, a precept is either positive or negative. If the person has been neglecting an obligation or duty, the precept will command the fulfillment of such an obligation by indicating what is to be done to curtail the commission of delicts. This is a positive precept. On the other hand, the subject matter of a precept may be the defendant's evil manner of acting, speaking, cohabiting, etc. He is thus commanded to omit such conduct. This is a negative precept.[218]

For both types of precepts, positive and negative, the law demands an accurate and precise expression of what is commanded, so that there will remain no danger of misunderstanding and no excuse for the otherwise contumacious offender.[219] Lega observes that this accuracy in indicating what is to be done or omitted is especially necessary because of the fact that the command is fortified with the sanction of a penalty.[220] Since a penalty will be inflicted upon the person if he is guilty of further transgression in the matter, justice would require that the person should be given a clear concept of exactly what conduct is expected of him.

3. *A Clear Threat of a Penalty to Which the Person Will be Subject in Case He Transgresses the Command*

The source of efficacy for the precept as a penal remedy resides in the coactive power of the Church.[221] By including a threat of an ecclesiastical penalty in case of disobedience to his command,[222] the Ordinary is able to utilize punishment in order to fortify his precept and better assure obedience to it. If the precept is disregarded, the penalty which results from this disobedience also binds in conscience.[223]

In giving a precept, the Ordinary may threaten either vindictive penalties or censures.[224] His choice will be guided to a great extent

218 Cf. Coronata, *Institutiones*, IV, 289, n. 1848; Sipos ennumerates the usual negative precepts: not conversing, not visiting, not retaining, not detaining.—*Enchiridion*, p. 853.

219 Cf. Ayrinhac-Lydon, *Penal Legislation*, p. 137, n. 182.

220 Cf. *Praelectiones*, IV, 360, n. 288.

221 Roelker, *Precepts*, p. 192.

222 C. 2310: . . . cum poenae comminatione in casu transgressionis.

223 Roelker, *Precepts*, p. 113.

224 Coronata, *Institutiones*, IV, 287, n. 1846.

by the type of delict and the characteristics of the person who is involved.[225] Whichever penalty the Ordinary decides upon, however, must be well defined and well determined in the precept.[226]

Roelker notes that before a precept is given, the entire matter should be weighed again and again so that a penalty which is threatened will neither be unjust nor too difficult to bear.[227] This view is in complete accord with canon 2241, § 2, which requires that no censure, especially *latae sententiae,* and particularly excommunication, should be inflicted except with serious and great circumspection.[228] Although there is not a similar canon concerning the sobriety which should direct the imposition of vindictive penalties, the Code's citation of the Council of Trent, that severity should be tempered with mildness, must always be kept in mind as a guide for the Ordinary who is faced with the obligation of imposing precepts.[229]

Within the limits of prudence and serious circumspection, the Ordinary may fortify his command with the threat either of an apt vindictive penalty or censure. While these penalties may be either *latae* or *ferendae sententiae,* it should be remembered that such penalties are presumed to be *ferendae sententiae* unless the opposite is clearly and expressly determined in the wording of the precept.[230] It is thought that normally a *ferendae sententiae* penalty would best be employed in a precept, with the *latae sententiae* penalty being relied upon only for a more serious crime. On this point, Roelker cites the counsel of Pope Benedict XIV [1740-1758] against the free use of *latae sententiae* penalties, and declares that this position is still the doctrine and the spirit of the Code of Canon Law.[231]

225 Lega, *Praelectiones,* IV, 360, n. 289.

226 Ayrinhac-Lydon, *Penal Legislation,* p. 137, n. 182; Lega, *Praelectiones,* IV, 360, n. 288; Coronata, *Institutiones,* IV, 287, n. 1846.

227 *Precepts,* p. 174.

228 C. 2241, § 2: Censurae, praesertim latae sententiae, maxime excommunicatio, ne infligantur, nisi sobrie et magna cum circumspectione.

229 Cf. c. 2214, § 2.

230 Cf. c. 2217, § 2.

231 *Precepts,* pp. 174-175.

SCHOLION. A TIME LIMIT IN THE PRECEPT

Besides the command to do or avoid something and the threat of a penalty for disobedience, some precepts should contain a fixed time limit.[232] This establishment of a specified time limit would, of course, depend upon the nature of the crime involved.

In the case of a positive precept, a determined time limit within which the command is to be fulfilled, is in order.[233] Depending upon the wording of the precept, the person who has not complied by the end of a specified time either *ipso facto* incurs the penalty which has been threatened, or else is subject to receive a *ferendae sententiae* penalty. It is thought, however, that such a specification of time is not *per se* essential to a precept, but only useful in order to add urgency to the obligation of obedience to the command. A time limit is especially seen to be unnecessary in regard to negative precepts.[234]

The inclusion of a definite time limit before the penalty is inflicted depends, therefore, upon the type of delinquency which is being prevented or repressed, and the particular circumstances attached thereto. It should be noted that since the nature of a precept demands that it be honest, just, and morally possible to fulfill,[235] even if no lapse of time is specified in the precept, it is understood that a reasonable amount of time would be allowed for the person to obey the command. The law is understood to be reasonable and does not intend to require what is morally impossible. Since the purpose of the command in the precept is to elicit the obedience and cooperation of the person who is being corrected, it is only reasonable that he be allowed sufficient time to cooperate, whether a time limit is specified or not.[236] It is indeed traditional that there should be a sufficient and reasonable interval of time between the giving of an admonition or a precept and the subsequent imposition of penalties in consequence of continued disobedience.[237]

232 Cf. Lega, *Praelectiones*, IV, 360, n. 288.

233 Cf. Cocchi, *Commentarium*, VIII, 210, n. 124.

234 Cf. Coronata, *Institutiones*, IV, 289, n. 1848.

235 Cf. Roelker, *Precepts*, p. 74.

236 Cf. Coronata, *Institutiones*, IV, 289, n. 1848.

237 Cf. c. 26, X, *de appellationibus, recusationibus et relationibus*, II,

At the same time, it is understood that the Ordinary cannot conscientiously permit an interminable delay and disregard for his precepts. He must threrefore inflict a penalty after a reasonable lapse of time. It is left to his prudent judgment to determine what lapse of time is reasonable.

SECTION B. THE USE OF THE PRECEPT

Canon 2310 deals with the use of the precept as a penal remedy. According to this canon, when warnings and rebukes have been made in vain, or if there seems to be no reason to hope for effect through their use, a precept should be given.[238] Since the precept is a more severe penal remedy than warning and rebuke, it should regularly be used only after they have been tried, and have been found to be useless or ineffective.[239] In the pre-Code legislation, the normal procedure was for warnings to precede the use of the precept, and the latter was employed only after the warnings were found to be fruitless and given in vain.[240] Coronata believes that this procedure is still the general norm which the Code presents to be followed.[241]

When is a warning or rebuke considered to have been given in vain? A general answer to this, of course, would be that they are always useless or given in vain when they fail to achieve the crime-prevention or preventive-repressive objective for which they were given. More specific signs are pointed out in relation to the judicial rebuke by Vermeersch-Creusen. These authors quote canon 1953 to the effect that the rebuke is considered useless if the

28; c. 4, X, *de cohabitatione clericorum et mulierum,* III, 2; c. 13, X, *de poenis,* V, 37; c. 17, X, *de testamentis et ultimis voluntatibus,* III, 26; Hostiensis, *Commentaria,* II, 178; III, 83.

238 C. 2310: Monitionibus et correptionibus incassum factis, vel si ex eisdem effectum sperare non liceat, datur praeceptum, . . . cf. also Regatillo, *Institutiones,* II, 532, n. 960; Cocchi, *Commentarium,* VIII, 210, n. 124.

239 Cf. Ayrinhac-Lydon, *Penal Legislation,* p. 138, n. 182; Vermeersch-Creusen, *Epitome,* III, 309, n. 504.

240 *Sacra Haec,* n. 7: Quatenus infructuosae monitiones evadunt, Ordinarius praecipit curiae, ut delinquenti analogum iniungatur praeceptum . . . ; *Cum Magnopere,* n. VII: Quod si monitiones in irritum cedant, Ordinarius iubet, per curiam delinquenti analogum praeceptum intimari . . .

241 *Institutiones,* IV, 288, n. 1847.

defendant does not accept the remedies, pious works, and penances which are prescribed for him, or having accepted them, he does not fulfill them.[242] This seems to be an acceptable criterion for both the warning and the rebuke. One may say, therefore, that warnings and rebukes are given in vain if the accused person refuses to accept them, or if he neglects to follow what they indicated he should do.[243]

Besides providing for the preliminary use of the warning and rebuke before issuing a precept, the present legislation also allows that, if the Ordinary knows the circumstances of the case or the character of the person are of such a nature that there is no hope the warning and rebuke will be effective, he may by-pass them and immediately use the precept.[244] The decision whether or not the preliminary use of the warning and rebuke is necessary is left to the judgment of the Ordinary who will impose the precept.[245]

In making the decision concerning the use of the precept the Ordinary should not be too ready to despair of the fruitful use of the warning and rebuke. Every reasonable use of the milder measures should be attempted before the precept is imposed. On this point, Roelker observes that there are many occasions when a warning will suffice to obtain the desired reform, and the use of the precept in such cases would be entirely improper although it would require obedience if so given.[246]

There are other times, of course, when the actions of men do not permit any hope of real improvement unless a direct command is given to them. In these latter cases the Ordinary may immediately resort to use the precept. Berutti notes that the decision to employ the precept immediately is made considerably easier if there is already a case which urges action because of the grave necessity of repairing scandal, or if the accused has often been guilty of evil conduct.[247]

In general, it may therefore be said that conditions must fully

[242] *Epitome,* III, 140, n. 270.

[243] Cf. Berutti, *Institutiones,* VI, 243, n. 97.

[244] Vermeersch-Creusen, *Epitome,* III, 309, n. 504; Ayrinhac-Lydon, *Penal Legislation,* p. 138, n. 182; Jone, *Commentarium,* III, 493.

[245] Coronata, *Institutiones,* IV, 288, n. 1848.

[246] Cf. *Precepts,* p. 196.

[247] Cf. *Institutiones,* VI, 243, n. 97.

indicate the presence of the legal requirements for the use of the precept.[248] These requirements are that: 1) warnings and rebukes have first been given and have proven ineffective; or 2) the circumstances of the case leave no reasonable hope that, if they were used, they would be effective. In one situation the precept is used as a subsequent and more severe remedy; in the other the precept is employed first because it is seen to be the only apt measure to be effective.

When one considers what types of cases may involve the use of the precept, he is aware that the scope of this penal remedy is quite extensive.

First of all it is evident that the precept may be used in cases where the subject matter is a delict which is certain. Such an application of the precept is in accord with the provisions of canon 1933, § 4 concerning the extra-judicial use of the penal remedies. This canon allows that, as long as there is a certain delict, the penal remedies may be imposed extra-judicially to the individuals involved.[249]

When a delict which is certain is the subject matter of a case, the precept is given for the preventive-repressive objective of the penal remedies. The precept, used in this way, is not a preventive penal remedy except in regard to the commission of future crimes.[250] Since such a precept is given only after a careful investigation has resulted in satisfactory proof of the existence of the crime, it really may be considered equivalent to a condemnatory sentence which has been conditionally suspended.[251] The infliction of the threatened penalty is thus conditional upon the subsequent obedience or transgression of the command in the precept.

Secondly, besides the use of the precept for delicts which have already been committed and are certain, it is equally evident that the use of the precept extends to other cases as well. Indeed, the

[248] Jone, *Commentarium*, III, 493.

[249] C. 1933, § 4: Poenitentia, remedium poenale, excommunicatio, suspensio, interdictum, dummodo delictum certum sit, infligi possunt etiam per modum praecepti extra iudicium.

[250] Roelker, *Precepts*, p. 195.

[251] DeMeester, *Compendium*, p. 230, n. 1805; Roelker, *Precepts*, p. 195; Cocchi, *Commentarium*, VIII, 210, n. 124.

whole mentality of crime-prevention which underlies the existence and application of the penal remedies calls for the precept to be used in such a manner that it is not limited to delicts which are certain. This extensive application is verified by canon 2310, which provides that: 1) Whenever the warning and rebuke have been given in vain, the precept should be given; 2) Whenever it is judged that, for any case the use of the warning and rebuke is without hope of being effective, the precept may immediately be given.[252] Under the conditions specified by canon 2310, therefore, the subject matter for the use of the precept may properly include the cases comprehended by both canon 2307 and canon 2308 for the warning and rebuke—cases when a delict has not yet been committed or when there is no certainty of its commission.

Roelker calls attention to the extensive use of the precept as a penal remedy. After recalling the preventive role of the penal remedies as contained in the pre-Code Instructions, *Sacra Haec* and *Cum Magnopere,* he states that:

> . . . while the use of a precept after a crime is committed to guard against future crimes must be considered as contained in canon 2310, it must likewise be asserted that this is not its principal purpose. The principal purpose of the precept as a penal remedy is to prevent even the first crime.[253]

Several other authors are in accord with the views concerning the use of the precept as discussed above. While Coronata alludes to canon 1933, § 4 as having a connection with the use of the precept,[254] he nevertheless allows the precept to be used in cases involving: the giving of scandal, the proximate occasion of committing a delict, the grave disturbing of order, provided a summary knowledge of the facts is had beforehand and proof obtained.[255] Berutti likewise states that a precept may be used against someone

[252] C. 2310: Monitionibus et correptionibus incassum factis, vel si ex eisdem effectum sperare non liceat, datur praeceptum, ...

[253] *Precepts,* pp. 195-196.

[254] *Institutiones,* IV, 287, n. 1846.

[255] *Institutiones,* IV, 288, n. 1846. He is not willing, however, to allow a precept to be given for a mere suspicion of having committed a delict, unless this is also connected with the danger of committing a delict—cf. p. 288, note 5.

who already has certainly committed a delict, or certainly appears to be in the proximate occasion of committing a delict.[256]

The present writer sees nothing contradictory or objectionable to the use of the precept even for those cases where an investigation leaves a grave suspicion that a crime has been committed. In such cases, it seems that the defendant should be given every opportunity to present his defense. If the grave suspicion still remains, the Ordinary could, without imputing blame for the past, issue a command as to what is to be done or avoided and threaten a penalty if his command is disobeyed. The Ordinary is thus employing the precept as a preventive remedy, trying to forestall scandal and to remove the person from the occasion of delinquency. As long as the evidence is of such a nature that the Ordinary prudently judges that there is a grave suspicion that a delict was committed, he can take steps to see that such a situation does not happen again.

SECTION C. THE FORM FOR IMPOSING THE PRECEPT

While canon 2310 specifies that the precept must accurately indicate to the person being corrected what is to be done or avoided, and also provides for the threat of a penalty to be included, there is no mention of a special form or specific manner in which the precept is to be given. The canon merely states that the precept is to be given.[257]

In the absence of a specification how the penal remedy of precept is to be applied, it is reasonable to presume that the regulations of the Code concerning precepts in general and the imposition of penalties by particular precepts must be followed. It is thought also that the pattern for giving the canonical remedy of precept in the pre-Code legislation should be considered in order to determine how much of it still has application today.

The legislation of the Code concerning precepts in general does not require any special form for the valid imposition of a precept.[258] The personal obligation of obedience results as soon as the command is made known to the person being commanded. A precept, given orally and privately (i. e. with no witnesses or memorandum

256 *Institutiones,* VI, 242, n. 97.

257 C. 2310: . . . datur praeceptum, ...

258 Cf. Roelker, *Precepts,* p. 23.

whatsoever) carries with it an obligation to obey what has been commanded. It binds the one to whom it is given everywhere he might go.[259]

If, however, certain qualities are desired to be imparted to a precept, then definite requirements or specifications of the law must be observed. Thus, precepts are by their nature presumed to be temporary unless the contrary can be demonstrated.[260] They can be made permanent by the Ordinary, but this permanence must be established and is not presumed. Unless proper steps are taken to make it permanent, the precept simply, definitely and completely ceases when the Superior who imposed it ceases in office.[261] As Roelker observes, oral precepts retain their validity as long as the Superior retains his office, but, "It is impossible today, however, for a Superior to insist that his precept is permanent, unless he has followed the prescriptions of canon 24." [262]

Precepts are likewise presumed to be private. They cannot be judicially enforced unless proper measures are employed to make them apt material for judicial procedure.[263]

When giving any precept, therefore, the provisions of canon 24 must be kept in mind. This canon supplies the means both for making a precept endure after the Superior who imposed it ceases in office, and for making it able to be judicially enforced. Canon 24 states that precepts which are given to individuals oblige those to whom they are given, wherever they may go, but they cannot be judicially enforced, and they cease when the one who imposed them ceases in office, unless they are imposed either by legitimate document or before two witnesses.[264] Thus, in order to assure the continuance of a precept after the one who imposed it ceases in office, one of two ways are specified by the law. The precept must be given either: 1) by means of a legitimate document, or 2) before

259 C. 24: Praecepta, singulis data, eos quibus dantur, ubique urgent, . . . ; cf. Sipos, *Enchiridion*, p. 853.

260 Roelker, *Precepts*, p. 99; p. 21.

261 *Ad mentem* c. 24.

262 *Precepts*, p. 99.

263 Cf. Berutti, *Institutiones*, VI, 243, n. 97.

264 C. 24: Praecepta, singulis data, eos quibus dantur, ubique urgent, sed judicialiter urgeri nequeunt et cessant resoluto iure praecipientis, nisi per legitimum documentum aut coram duobus testibus imposita fuerint.

two witnesses.[265] If, on the other hand, it is desired to give a precept in such a manner that it can be judicially enforced, the precept is also made capable of strict judicial proof [266] by employing either of the above mentioned methods.[267]

In passing, it may be recalled here that besides canon 24, the provisions of canon 2225 must likewise be remembered when there is a question either of a declaratory sentence or the actual imposing of a penalty by precept. This canon states that if a *latae* or *ferendae sententiae* penalty has been inflicted, threatened, *ad modum praecepti particularis,* ordinarily the subsequent declaratory sentence or imposing of the penalty must be made either in writing or before two witnesses, giving an indication of the cause of the penalty (except in the process *ex informata conscientiae* of canon 2193).[268]

By following the prescripts of canon 2225 in the imposing of the actual penalty by particular precept and giving it either in writing or before two witnesses, the permanence of the penalty by precept as provided for by canon 24 is obtained. Whether or not the precept could be judicially enforced, however, would further depend upon the legitimacy of the document which was used,[269] or the qualification of the witnesses which the Code demands in order that they might be acceptable to give judicial testimony.[270]

As for what constitutes the legitimate document required by canon 24, it seems that a private document would be sufficient to effect the continuance of the precept after the Ordinary ceased juridically to occupy his office.[271] In order that a precept may be judicially enforced by documentary proof, it would be most desirable, if not absolutely necessary, that the document follow the

265 DeMeester, *Compendium,* p. 231, n. 1805.

266 Bouscaren-Ellis, *Canon Law,* p. 36.

267 Blat, *Commentarium,* V ,192, n. 144.

268 C. 2225: . . . si vero poena latae vel ferendae sententiae inflicta sit ad modum praecepti particularis, scripto aut coram duobus testibus ordinarie declaretur vel irrogetur, indicatis poenae causis, salvo praescripto can. 2193.

269 C. 24: . . . per legitimum documentum. . . .

270 Cf. cc. 1756-1758.

271 Cf. Roelker, *Precepts,* p. 100.

prescriptions of canon 1813, § 1, 1° and be signed either by the Ordinary or a notary, thus becoming a public document.[272]

Canon 24 also provides for the presence of two witnesses.[273] Since their purpose in being present is to witness the fact that the precept is being given, there seem to be no special qualities of acceptability or character required to fulfill the role of witness here. Anyone whose presence and alertness are such that he experiences the fact that a precept is being given, would qualify in this regard. Such presence while the precept is being given effects permanence in the duration of the precept.

In order that the presence of witnesses would also assure the fact that the precept could be judicially enforced, the canons relative to the admissibility of witnesses must be considered.[274] The possibility of subsequent judicial action would therefore require that one be prudent and selective in his choice of witnesses to a precept, so that later they would be acceptable to give *prima facie* judicial testimony, if such action is necessary. Otherwise the testimony of witnesses who are judicially unsuitable or suspect could at most give adminicular proof of the precept, if an effort were made to have it judicially enforced.[275] Having given attention to the legislation of the Code regarding precepts in general in canon 24, it is well now to recall also the pre-Code law concerning the canonical remedy of precept.

Both of the pre-Code Instructions, *Sacra Haec* and *Cum Magnopere,* provided for a definite method of giving the precept. After a careful inquiry established the need of employing the canonical remedies, the warning was to be given.[276] If the warning failed to produce its intended effect, the Ordinary was to order his curia to give the delinquent a precept about the matter, in which it was explained what he was to do or avoid, together with the threat of an ecclesiastical penalty which he would incur if he transgressed the precept.[277] This precept was to be given to the delinquent by

[272] *Ad mentem* c. 1816, a public document gives faith to those things which are directly and principally affirmed in it.

[273] C. 24: . . . aut coram duobus testibus. . . .

[274] Cf. cc. 1756-1758.

[275] Cf. c. 1758.

[276] *Sacra Haec,* n. 6; *Cum Magnopere,* n. VI.

[277] *Sacra Haec,* n. 7; *Cum Magnopere,* n. VII.

the chancellor of the curia in the presence of either the Vicar General or two witnesses who could be clerics or laymen of proven merit.[278] A record of giving the precept was to be signed by the parties who were present, including the delinquent if he wished to do so.[279] If it was prudently seen that the nature of the case required the observance of secrecy, the Vicar General could impose an oath of secrecy about the matter.[280]

The Third Plenary Council of Baltimore gave emphasis to the legislation of *Cum Magnopere* by repeating number VII and sections 1° and 2° of number VIII of this Instruction. It did not, however, promulgate any further particular law for this country by making further specifications on the matter of the precept.[281]

In the light of canon 2310, together with canon 24, one may appraise the value of the pre-Code leglislation upon the giving of the penal remedy of precept today. Because of similiarity in both Instructions, reference will be made only to the numbering as it appears in *Cum Magnopere,* although it applies to *Sacra Haec* as well.

1. Canon 2310 gives greater latitude to the Ordinary in so far as he may by-pass the warning if he judges that it will not be effective. When the conditions warrant it, therefore, the Ordinary is not required to defer to the formality of giving the warning, but may proceed with the giving of the precept immediately. The provision of number VI need not be followed.

2. Canon 2310 and number VII of *Cum Magnopere* provide that the precept is to indicate what is to be done or avoided by the person to whom it is issued, and that a penalty which would be incurred for transgressing the precept is to be threatened at the same time. This provision of number VII remains in force.

3. Neither canon 2310 nor canon 24 give any indication that the curia is to issue the precept. The presumption would be that the Ordinary may follow the same pattern as is outlined by canons 2307 and 2308 for the warning and the rebuke, i. e. the Ordinary

278 *Sacra Haec,* n. 8; *Cum Magnopere,* n. VIII.

279 *Sacra Haec,* n. 8, 1°; *Cum Magnopere,* n. VIII, 1°.

280 *Sacra Haec,* n. 8, 2°; *Cum Magnopere,* n. VIII, 2°.

281 Cf. Conc. Pl. Balt. III., n. 309—*Acta et Decreta,* p. 177.

may proceed *per se vel per interpositam personam.* While the Ordinary may choose to impose a precept by using his curia, he is not obliged to do so. Number VIII no longer obliges, but may be followed if the Ordinary chooses to do so.

4. In order to place the delinquent under the obligation of obedience, canon 24 does not require that the precept must be given before the Vicar General or two witnesses. This provision of number VIII need not be followed.

5. When witnesses are used in accord with canon 24 there must be two witnesses. The presence of only the Vicar General will not suffice. If it is desired to make the precept permanent or judicially enforceable, this provision of number VIII may not be followed.

6. Neither canon 2310 nor canon 24 requires that witnesses must be used in giving a precept; therefore, their signatures cannot be necessary for the giving of the precept. When witnesses are used, their signature would be useful, but it seems that it is not necessary for the legal value of the precept. The provision of number VIII, 1° may at times be useful, but need not be followed.

7. Nothing in the present law requires that the person to whom the precept is given must sign it. Such a signature was optional to the delinquent in the Instructions. This provision of number VIII, 1° may be followed today, but still remains optional.

8. The present legislation makes no mention about requiring an oath of secrecy regarding the issuance of a precept or the subject matter involved. The Ordinary may certainly require such an oath if he prudently judges it to be necessary. The provision of number VIII, 2°, making the oath of secrecy contingent upon the prudent judgment of its necessity, still must be followed.

9. Since the presence of the Vicar General is in no manner required by the present legislation for the giving of the precept, it is unreasonable to suppose that he must nonetheless be present to impose the oath of secrecy if it is to be used. This provision of number VIII, 2° need not be followed.

The preceding considerations of the present legislation on precepts in general, and the pre-Code Instructions on the canonical remedy of precept, serve to crystallize the concepts of how the penal remedy of precept may be imposed today. With these concepts as a background, the form for issuing the precept may now be given attention.

Since the provisions of canon 24 do not demand the use of a document or witnesses for a legitimate precept, the penal remedy of precept may be given orally with no witnesses present, and it still imposes an obligation of obedience to its command upon the person to whom it is given. Such a precept will endure as long as the Ordinary who imposes it remains in office, unless he specifies a shorter period of time for its duration. Because it is inflicted without a legitimate document and without witnesses, such a precept cannot be judicially enforced.

If the Ordinary wishes his precept to have permanence beyond his tenure of office or to be capable of judicial enforcement, then the further specifications of canon 24 regarding the use of a legitimate document or two witnesses must be followed.

Furthermore, it may be noted that since a record or memorandum must be made and preserved in the secret archives whenever the warning or rebuke is given,[282] so *a fortiori,* the same practice should be followed in regard to the precept also.[283] Such a document would properly enable the Ordinary to give an account of his action if it is questioned by higher authority. A *post factum* memorandum to the effect that a precept had previously been issued would not, however, make the precept permanent or judicially enforceable. For such results, canon 24 requires that the precept must actually be inflicted or imposed by the legitimate document in question.[284]

Article VI. Surveillance (*Vigilantia*)

Surveillance was not listed among the canonical preventive measures of the pre-Code Instructions,[285] but was first introduced as a penal remedy in the Code of Canon Law.[286]

At the present time, it would indeed be an understatement to observe that the exact length and breath of the concept of surveil-

282 C. 2309, § 5.

283 Lega-Bartocetti, *Commentarius in Iudicia Ecclesiastica* (3 vols., Romae: Azienda Libraria Cattolica Italiana, 1950), III, 196.

284 C. 24: . . . nisi per legitimum documentum . . . imposita fuerint.

285 Cf. *Sacra Haec,* n. 4; *Cum Magnopere,* n. IV.

286 Coronata, *Institutiones,* IV, 289, n. 1849.

lance is still ill-defined. A study of the Code and the authors give some indication of the application of this remedy, but the cumulative effect of this study produces little more than a sketchy notion of what surveillance is, and how it is distinguished from canonical entities which are similar to, but are not surveillance. The present writer makes no pretentions of having solved this difficulty, but attempts here to present a sufficiently unified notion of surveillance in order that this inter-relation and application of the penal remedies in general may be understood.

While it is the duty of the Ordinary to watch over the faith and morals of each member of his flock and the general status of that portion of the Church which is entrusted to his care, the vigilance which constitutes the penal remedy of surveillance is a special and particularly confined type of watchfulness.[287]

Basically surveillance is the penal remedy by which the Ordinary places someone under the special watchfulness, vigilance, or custody of himself or some specified person.[288] Ayrinhac-Lydon state that this measure of discipline is to be considered as an exceptional remedy in so far as it should be used only in exceptional and grave cases, particularly when there is some serious reason to fear relapses into evil conduct.[289] Certainly it must be agreed that any measure which in some manner and to some degree subjects anyone to the watchfulness of another person must be used with moderation, because it involves a lessening of liberty as well as a possible lessening of the good name or honor of the person who is thus corrected.[290] Even though this remedy is able to be employed with the help of a prudent priest who maintains secrecy in the matter, Cocchi observes that such undesirable effects can result from being subjected to surveillance, that he insists upon moderation in its use.[291]

287 Cf. Ayrinhac-Lydon, *Penal Legislation*, p. 139, n. 184.

288 Cf. Coronata, *Institutiones*, IV, 289, n. 1849.

289 *Penal Legislation*, p. 139, n. 184.

290 Cf. Blat, *Commentarium*, V, 192, n. 145; Berutti, *Institutiones*, VI, 244, n. 98; Vermeersch-Creusen, *Epitome*, III, 309, n. 505; DeMeester, *Compendium*, p. 231, n. 1806.

291 *Commentarium*, VIII, 210, n. 125.

SECTION A. TYPES OF SURVEILLANCE

In view of the fact that the subjection of one person to the watchfulness of another is the basic concept of surveillance, it is possible that this remedy may exist in several different species or forms. Because these forms differ among themselves in degrees of severity, the gravity of a particular case should guide the Ordinary or judge in his decision of which form is to be used in any one case. Since surveillance is imposed either by an Ordinary [292] or a judge,[293] it is apparent that it is they who must decide not only when the gravity of a case warrants the use of this remedy, but also what form of surveillance is to be imposed upon the delinquent.

In its mildest form, it seems that surveillance could involve complete freedom of legitimate movement in society except for the obligation of reporting to a custodian at specified intervals of time. The purpose of these periodic reports is to verify the delinquent's stability in avoiding a relapse into his delictual conduct. This type of surveillance would be employed where the weakness of the delinquent's character, rather than the circumstances of some place or particular person, is the source of danger for a relapse into crime.

For cases involving circumstances where a certain place or places are the occasion of the danger of a relapse into delinquency, the curtailment of freedom is more extensive. As Cocchi points out, if the delinquent is in danger of lapsing into the same crime because of the circumstances of some place, the best remedy is to remove him from that place and put him under vigilance lest he may go to that place again.[294]

The authors present several aspects of this second type of surveillance, stating that it may involve an order to: 1) remain in a certain place; [295] 2) keep away from a certain place;[296] 3)

292 C. 2311, § 1.

293 C. 2234.

294 *Commentarium,* VIII, 210, n. 125.

295 Vermeersch-Creusen, *Epitome,* III, 309, n. 505; Cocchi, *Commentarium,* VIII, 210, n. 125.

296 *Ibid.*

withdraw from a certain place;[297] and 4) withdraw to an appointed place.[298] To each of these possibilities is added the requirement that the delinquent must present himself to the Ordinary or his delegate at determined intervals of time. In this manner, the delinquent is removed from the place where he finds the occasion of delinquency and also, by some privation of his freedom, his capriciousness is checked.[299]

Here it may be observed that, frequently enough, the exercise of surveillance will be entrusted by the Ordinary to a delegate who is chosen for his prudence, wisdom and beneficial influence upon people. The Vicar General, rural dean, or pastor may well be chosen for this assignment. It is clear, of course, that when a delegate is employed, the delinquent's obligation of obedience remains the same as if the surveillance were exercised by the Ordinary himself.[300]

The types of surveillance considered thus far, while limiting somewhat the activity of the delinquent, have nevertheless left him to enjoy a considerable amount of freedom. There is quite a wide amount of liberty still open to him, in spite of the fact that he must avoid certain places and report to his custodian from time to time. Since references by the authors[301] to these aspects of surveillance are frequent, one may possibly conclude that this is the extent of the curtailment of freedom which is permissible in the use of the penal remedy of surveillance. At least two authors, however, allude to a more strict type of surveillance which involves greater confinement of the delinquent.

Berutti presents an example whereby the delinquent is not permitted to leave from his habitual place of living, except by permission of the approved person in whose particular care he has been entrusted.[302] Sipos likewise refers to a delinquent being sent to a monastery or seminary as an example of surveillance.[303] The

[297] Sipos, *Enchiridion,* p. 853.

[298] *Ibid.*

[299] Vermeersch-Creusen, *Epitome,* III, 309, 505.

[300] Cf. Sipos, *Enchiridion,* p. 854.

[301] E. g. Cocchi, Vermeersch-Creusen, and Sipos.

[302] *Institutiones,* VI, 244, n. 98.

[303] *Enchiridion,* p. 854.

intention here is, of course, not to be a monk or a seminarian, but rather to live at these establishments for a time under the surveillance of the rector or someone duly appointed for the task. This latter procedure is a very drastic measure. While no one would deny that this form of discipline is a very effective method of preventing the commission of certain delicts, such action would seem often enough to be a vindictive penalty or a penance rather than a penal remedy. Initiated with the proper motivation which is specific to the penal remedies, however, it is conceivable that even such drastic action could aptly be considered as a grave type of surveillance. It may be recalled here that surveillance shares the two-fold preventive and repressive objectives or motives of all penal remedies:[304] 1) preventive—to prevent evils, forestall scandal, remove voluntary occasions and all proximate causes of delinquency; 2) repressive—to help the delinquent regain a sense of duty and to repair the evil effects of his crimes.[305] Thus, confinement for either of these objectives can be considered as the penal remedy of surveillance.

SECTION B. THE USE OF SURVEILLANCE

1. *The Danger of Relapsing into a Crime*

When one reads canon 2311, § 1, two different interpretations of when surveillance may be used suggest themselves.[306]

The first interpretation emphasizes the presence of a *casus gravitas,* with the effect that whenever there is a grave case, even if the person has never previously been guilty of a delict, surveillance may be employed. This interpretation considers the remainder of canon 2311, § 1 to merely contain an indication of those times when special reasons are present for imposing surveillance, viz. especially when a person is in danger of relapsing into the same crime. The possibility of quite widespread use of this remedy could be allowed by this interpretation.

The second interpretation of canon 2311, § 1 considers the com-

[304] Cf. Blat, *Commentarium,* V, 192, n. 145.

[305] *Sacra Haec,* n. 2.

[306] C. 2311, § 1: Si casus gravitas ferat et praecipue si agatur de eo qui in periculo versatur relabendi in idem crimen, eum Ordinarius submittat vigilantiae.

mission of a previous crime as a prime requisite for the existence of any gravity which would be sufficient for the use of surveillance. This view maintains that the term *relabendi* must be understood to govern any use of this remedy, i. e. surveillance may be used only when a crime has been committed, and the gravity of the present case includes the danger of *relapsing* into delinquency.[307] According to this view, the term *praecipue* as used in the canon refers merely to a relapse into the *same crime,* and does not impart a qualification upon the whole clause in the canon.[308] The canon would thus be interpreted to mean that whenever there is danger of relapsing into crime, and *especially* when there is danger of relapsing into the *same crime,* if the gravity of the case warrants it, the Ordinary should submit the person to surveillance. This second interpretation would involve a more limited use of surveillance.

In the absence of an authentic interpretation of the exact meaning of canon 2311, § 1, it seems that justification could be found for following either interpretation for the employment of surveillance. However, the present writer holds that the force of canon 2219 [309] obliges here, and that the view which presents the more limited use of surveillance would thus have to be followed. It is the opinion of the present writer that the penal remedy of surveillance may be employed only when a person has already committed a delict and there is, moreover, a grave danger of his relapsing into crime, i. e. danger of a delinquent becoming at least a second-offender. The use of *praecipue* in canon 2311, § 1 emphasizes the use of surveillance when the danger involves the same species of crime as was committed before, but allows also for its use when there is danger of a crime of some other kind.

[307] Coronata presents the opinion that in order for anyone to be subjected to surveillance, the Ordinary must have proof of two conditions: 1) the person must already have committed a crime; and 2) at the same time there must also exist the danger of lapsing again into the same crime. He admits, however, that the use of *praecipue* in canon 2311, § 1 permits surveillance to be used in other cases as well; but he gives no indication what these other cases may involve—cf. *Institutiones,* IV, 289-290, n. 1849.

[308] C. 2311, § 1: . . . et praecipue si agatur de eo qui in periculo versatur relabendi in idem crimen. . . .

[309] C. 2219: In poenis benignior est interpretatio facienda.

2. *A Grave Case*

The use of the penal remedy of surveillance is always contingent upon the existence of a case which is grave enough to warrant employing such measures which involve both the limitation of liberty and the possible decline of the good name [310] of the person upon whom it is inflicted. Since it is the task of the Ordinary or the judge to impose this remedy,[311] it must likewise be their duty to determine when the gravity of a case requires or warrants its use.

Blat correctly points out that a case may be grave from one of two aspects: 1) because of the subject matter involved; or 2) due to the circumstances which accompany the subject matter.[312] When some very great delict or heinous crime has been committed, the case would certainly justify using that which may otherwise be considered as an extraordinary measure in order to avoid its repetition, which is seen to be a dangerous possibility. Likewise, the known circumstances of the existence of some extrinsic danger, or the internal element of the particular delinquent's weakness to certain types or places of temptation, may contribute such gravity to a case that the use of surveillance is seen to be necessary.

3. *Surveillance Used to Increase a Penalty*

Sometimes the use of surveillance has the aspect of being a means to increase a penalty.[313] The proper occasion for this use is verified when one considers the provision of canon 2234, to the effect that someone who has committed several delicts may be subjected to surveillance along with the regular punishment, if the judge prudently considers that such action is required.[314] Even though the several delicts committed were of different kind, the use of surveillance would thus be justified here because of the increased culpability involved.[315] For any particular case the

310 Cf. Vermeersch-Creusen, *Epitome*, III, 309, n. 505.

311 Cf. c. 2311, § 1; c. 2234.

312 *Commentarium*, V, 192, n. 145.

313 Cf. c. 2311, § 2: Vigilantia praecipi quoque potest ad augendam poenam, praecipue in recidivos.

314 C. 2234: Qui plura delicta commisit, non modo gravius puniri, sed si, prudenti iudicis arbitrio, res id ferat, subiici etiam debet vigilantiae vel alii remedio poenali.

315 *Ad mentem* c. 2208, § 2: Qui pluries deliquerit etiam diverso in genere, suam auget culpabilitatem.

decision for the use or non-use of surveillance as a means of increasing a penalty is left to the prudent appraisal of the case by the Ordinary or judge.

It is clear, moreover, that surveillance may be used to increase a penalty especially when a *recidivus* is involved.[316] A *recidivus,* according to legal terminology, here refers to someone who, subsequent to condemnation, again commits an offense of the same kind and under such circumstances (especially of time) that his steadfastness in ill-will is able to be prudently conjectured.[317] In order to qualify as a *recidivus,* there must have been a previous condemnation for the commission of a crime (Coronata notes that incurring a *latae sententiae* penalty would not suffice here, but rather there must have been an irrevocable condemnatory sentence).[318] There must also be a subsequent crime of the same kind committed in such a brief lapse of time after the condemnation that the stubborn ill-will of the delinquent is prudently judged to exist. Because of the delinquent's ill-will to perservere in crime, surveillance is used to augment the penalty which was incurred by the *recidivus* for his continued delictual conduct.

Even when surveillance is used to increase a penalty, the propriety of its serving as a preventive of future crime may not be overlooked.

SECTION C. THE FORM FOR IMPOSING SURVEILLANCE

The Code does not specify the manner in which surveillance may be imposed upon someone. In the absence of any special requirements, therefore, it seems that the prescripts of canon 2309 concerning the use of the warning and rebuke may be followed here also.[319] Thus, surveillance may be imposed secretly or publicly, the latter being given either judicially or extra-judicially. Whatever manner is employed for its application, a document relative to the subjection of a person to the penal remedy of surveillance should be kept in the secret archives.[320]

[316] C. 2311, § 2: . . . praecipue in recidivos.

[317] Cf. c. 2208, § 1.

[318] Cf. *Institutiones,* IV, 46, n. 1672.

[319] Cf. Jone, *Commentarium,* III, 493; Coronata, *Institutiones,* IV, 290, n. 1849.

[320] *Ad mentem* c. 2309, § 5.

CONCLUSIONS

CHAPTER I.

1. The foundation for the penal remedies of the Code is found at least implicitly in the Council of Trent, and explicitly in the Instructions *Sacra Haec* and *Cum Magnopere.*

2. In *Sacra Haec* and *Cum Magnopere* the preventive as well as the repressive remedies are given the status of canonical measures, and are, therefore, juridic methods of discipline in the external forum.

3. The canonical remedy of warning in the pre-Code legislation did not include an explicit threat of a penalty.

4. The precept of pre-Code legislation could threaten either a *ferendae* or *latae sententiae* penalty.

CHAPTER II.

1. The use of the penal remedies of the Code is an exercise of the power of jurisdiction proceeding from the public authority of the Ordinary.

2. The use of the penal remedies of the Code is limited to a competent Ordinary or ecclesiastical judge.

3. The competence of the Ordinary or judge to impose the penal remedies of the Code upon the proper subjects of the Ordinary is determined by a juridic relationship resulting from either a territorial or a personal bond. Competence over non-subjects comes from a territorial bond resulting from some specification of law.

4. The penal remedies of the Code may be issued both to the clergy and to the daity.

5. The penal remedies of the Code may be used as apt educative punishments prescribed by law for the correction of *impuberes.*

6. The penal remedies of the Code may be defined as: Moderate canonical measures of penal character, crime-preventive and preventive-repressive in nature, which are employed for cases specified

by law and imposed by a competent authority upon members of the Church to maintain its social order.

Chapter III.

1. While the group of the penal remedies as a legal entity or canonical institute possesses a definite characteristic of penality, and are very proximate to penalties, they are not true penalties in the strict sense of the definition in canon 2215. The penal remedies are *ad instar* penal.

2. The penal remedies are numbered among the official methods for punishing delinquents in the Church. They are specifically different from both the medicinal and the vindictive penalties.

Chapter IV.

1. Canon 2306 presents an exclusive list of the penal remedies of the Code.

2. Unless the circumstances which would warrant the use of the penal remedies of the Code are notorious or known certainly to exist by the Ordinary, a preliminary summary investigation of the matter must precede any use of the remedies.

3. In giving the warning, the topic of blame for the matter is by-passed; there is no threat of a specific penalty; the warning is made specifically to the person being warned; and the Ordinary is indicated as the author of the warning.

4. A record of every penal remedy must be kept in the secret archives of the curia.

5. The rebuke emphasizes the element of culpability for the commission of a delict or grave misconduct.

6. The penal remedy of precept is a type of particular penal precept.

7. The precept contains three essential elements: 1) A command given by a competent authority; 2) An accurate indication of what is to be done or avoided by the person to whom the command is given; 3) A clear threat of an ecclesiastical penalty to which the person will be subject in case he transgresses the command.

8. Most of the formalities prescribed by the pre-Code legislation for the giving of the precept have been abrogated by the Code.

9. As a penal remedy, the precept may be given orally and without witnesses, or else it may be given either before two witnesses or in writing. The latter methods are the normal manner of procedure in the actual execution or declaration of penalty upon the transgression of the penal precept in accord with canon 2225.

10. To impart permanence to the precept, or to make it judicially enforceable, canon 24 must be followed.

11. Basically, surveillance is the penal remedy by which the Ordinary places someone under the special watchfulness, vigilance, or custody of himself or some other specified person.

12. Surveillance may be employed only when a person has already committed a delict and there is, moreover, a grave case involving the danger of his relapsing again into crime.

APPENDIX

SACRA HAEC

(S. C. Ep. et Reg., instr. 11 iun. 1880.)

Sacra haec EE. et RR. Congregatio, mature praesenti Ecclesiae conditione perpensa, quae pene ubique impeditur, quominus externam explicet suam actionem super materias et personas ecclesiasticas, et considerato quoque defectu mediorum aptorum pro regulari curiarum ordinatione, constituit facultatem Ordinariis locorum expresse concedere, ut formas magis oeconomicas adhibere valeant in exercitio suae disciplinaris iurisdictionis super clericis. Ut autem tota iustitiae ratio sarta tectaque maneat, serveturque processuum canonica regularitas et uniformitas, opportunum censuit sequentes emenare normas, a curiis servandas.

1. Ordinario pastorale onus incumbit disciplinam correctionemque clericorum a se dependentium curandi, super eorumdem vitae rationem vigilando, remediisque utendo canonicis ad praecavendas apud eosdem et eliminandas ordinis perturbationes.

2. Ex his remediis alia praeveniunt, alia reprimunt et medelam afferunt Priora ad hoc diriguntur ut impediant quominus malum adveniat, ut scandali stimuli, occasiones voluntariae, causaeque ad delinquendum proximae removean-

CUM MAGNOPERE

(S. C. de Prop. Fide, instr. a. 1883.)

Cum magnopere huius S. Consilii intersit in ecclesiasticis iudiciis eam methodum servari quae et temporum circumstantiis opportune respondeat, et regulari iustitiae administrationi, nec non Praelatorum auctoritati tuendae, querelisque reorum praecavendis par omnino sit, placuit iterum ad examen revocari ea omnia quae in hac re pro eclesiis foederatorum Americae Septentrionalis Statuum in Instructione diei 20 iulii anno 1878, nec non in responsione ad dubia circa eamdem posterius proposita continebantur. Itaque S. C. omnibus mature perpensis, SSmo D. N. Leone PP. XIII approbante, haec quae sequuntur observanda decrevit, praecedenti instructione ac successiva declaratione abrogata, iis exceptis quae in hac continentur.

I. Ordinarius pro suo pastorali munere tenetur disciplinam correptionemque clericorum ita diligenter curare, ut circa eorum mores assidue vigilet, ac remedia a canonibus statuta sive praecavendis, sive tollendis abusibus in clerum aliquando irrepentibus provide adhibeat.

II. Haec vero remedia, alia *praeventiva* sunt alia *repressiva*. Illa quidem ad praepedienda mala, scandalorum stimulos amovendos; voluntarias occasiones et causas ad delinquendum proximas vitandas ordinantur. Haec vero eum in finem tur. Altera finem habent revocandi delinquentes ut sapiant reparentque admissi criminis consequentias.

3. Conscientiae et prudentiae Ordidarii horum remediorum incumbit applicatio, iuxta canonum praescriptiones, et casuum adiunctorumque gravitatem.

4. Mediis quae praeservant praecipue accensentur spiritualia exercitia, monitiones et praecepta.

5. Has provisiones praecedere debet summaria facti cognitio quae ab Ordinario notanda est, ut *ad ulteriora* procedere, quatenus opus sit, et certiorem redere queat superiorem auctoritatem, in casu legitimi recursus.

6. Canonicae monitiones fiunt sive in forma paterna et secreta (etiam per epistolam aut per interpositam personam) sive in forma legali, ita tamen ut de earumdem exercutione constet ex aliquo actu.

7. Quatenus infructuosae monitiones evadant, Ordinarius praecipit curiae, ut delinquenti analogum iniungatur praeceptum, in quo declaretur quid eidem agendum aut omittendum sit, cum respondentis poenae ecclesiasticae comminatione, quam incurret in casu transgressionis.

8. Praeceptum intimatur praevento a cancellario coram Vicario generali, sive coram duobus testibus ecclesiasticis aut laicis probatae integritatis.

§ 1. Actus subsignatur a partibus praesentibus et a praevento quoque, si velit.

constituta sunt, ut delinquentes ad bonam frugem revocentur, ac culparum consectaria e medio tollantur.

III. Conscientiae Ordinarii remittitur cuiusque remedii applicatio, canonicis praescriptionibus servatis pro casuum ac circumstantiarum gravitate.

IV. Praeventiva remedia sunt praecipue spiritualia exercitia, monitiones, praecepta.

V. Antequam vero adhibeantur, summaria factorum recognitio procedat oportet: cuius notitiam Ordinarius servari curet ut, si opus sit, ad ulteriora procedere possit, et ut auctoritatc ecclesiasticae superioris gradus in casu legitimi recursus totius rei rationem reddat.

VI. Canonicae monitiones vel secreto fiunt (etiam per epistolam vel per interpositam personam) ad modum paternae correptionis, vel servata forma legali adhibentur, ita tamen ut illarum exercutio ex aliquo actu pateat.

VII. Quod si monitiones in irritum cedant, Ordinarius iubet per Curiam delinquenti analogum praeceptum intimari ita, ut in hoc explicetur, quid ipse vel facere vel vitare debeat, addita respectivae poenae ecclesiasticae comminatione, quam, si praeceptum transgrediatur, incurret.

VIII. Praeceptum delinquenti a Curiae Cancellario coram Vicario generali iniungitur, aut etiam coram Vicario generali iniungitur, aut etiam coram duobus testibus ecclesiasticis, vel laicis spectatae probitatis.

1. Actus iniunctionis praecepti signatur a partibus praesentibus, et a delinquente etiam, si velit.

§ 2. Vicarius generalis adiicere valet iuramentum servandi secretum, quatenus id prudenter expetat tituli indoles, de quo agitur.

2. Vicarius Generalis iusiurandum testibus imponere potest de secreto servando, si prudenter a natura rei, de qua agitur, id requiratur.

9. Quoad *poenalia* media, animadvertant reverendissimi Ordinarii, praesenti instructione haud derogatum esse iudiciorum solemnitatibus, per sacros canones, per Apostolicas Constitutiones et alias ecclesiasticas dispositiones imperatis, quatenus eaedem libere efficaciterque applicari queant; sed oeconomicae formae consulere intendunt illis casibus curiisque, in quibus solemnes processus, aut adhiberi nequeant, aut non expedire videantur. Plenam quoque vim servat suam extrajudiciale remedium *ex informata conscientia* pro criminibus occultis, quod decrevit s. Tridentina Synodus in Sess. 14, cap. 1, de Reform. adhibendum, cum illis regulis et reservationibus, quas constanter servavit pro dicti Capitis interpretatione S. C. Congregatio in pluribus resolutionibus, et praecipue in *Bosnien.* et *Sirmien.* 20 Decembris 1873.

IX. Quod vero pertinet ad remedia repressiva seu poenas, animadvertant Ordinarii in suo pleno vigore manere remedium extraiudiciale ex informata conscientia pro occultis reatibus a S. Concilio Tridentino constitutum c. 1, Sess. 14, *de ref.*

BIBLIOGRAPHY

SOURCES

New Testament of Our Lord and Savior Jesus Christ, The, Confraternity edition, Paterson: St. Anthony Guild Press, 1941.

Acta Apostolicae Sedis, Commentarium Officiale, Romae, 1909-1929; Civitate Vaticana, 1929—.

Acta et Decreta Concilii Plenarii Baltimorensis Tertii, Baltimorae, 1886.

Acta Sanctae Sedis, 41 vols., Romae, 1865-1908.

Analecta Iuris Pontificii, Recueil des dissertations sur divers sujets de droit canonique, de liturgie, de theologie et d'histoire, 28 vols., Romae, Parisiis, Bruxellis, 1885-1891.

Bouscaren, T. Lincoln, *The Canon Law Digest*, 4 vols., Milwaukee: Bruce, 1934-1943-1953-1958.

Bruns, H. T., *Canones Apostolorum Conciliorum Saeculorum* IV-VII, 2 vols., Berolini, 1839.

Codex Iuris Canonici Pii X Pontificiis Maximi iussu digestus, Benedicti Papae XV auctoritate promulgatus, Praefatione, Fontium Annotatione et Indice Analytico-alphabetico ab Emo Petro Card. Gasparri auctus, Romae: Typis Polyglottis Vaticanis, 1917; reimpresso, 1933.

Codicis Iuris Canonici Fontes, cura Emi Petri Card. Gasparri editi, 9 vols., Romae [postea Civitate Vaticana]: Typis Polyglottis Vaticanis, 1923-1939 (Vols. VII-IX, ed. cura et studio Emi Iustiniani Card. Serédi).

Collectanea S. Congregationis de Propaganda Fide, 2 vols., Romae: Typographia Polyglotta S. C. de Propaganda Fide, 1907.

Corpus Iuris Canonici, ed. Lipsiensis II., post Aemilii Ludovici Richteri curas . . . instruxit Aemilius Friedberg, 2 vols., Lipsiae: Tauchnitz, 1879-1881; ad anastatice repetita, 1928.

Decretales D. Gregorii Papae IX, suae integritati una cum glossis restitutae, cum privilegio Gregorii XIII, Pont. Max., et Aliorum Principum, Romae, 1582.

Decretum Gratiani, emendatum et notationibus illustratum cum glossis, Gregorii XIII, Pont. Max., iussu editum, 2 vols., Romae, 1582.

Hardouin, Jean, *Acta Conciliorum et Epistolae Decretales ac Constitutiones Summorum Pontificum*, 12 vols., Parisiis, 1714-1715.

Jaffé, Phillipus, *Regesta Pontificum Romanorum ab condita Ecclesia ad annum post Christum natum MCXCVIII*, 2. ed., correctam et auctam auspiciis G. Wattenbach, curaverunt S. Loewenfeld, F. Kaltenbrunner, P. Ewald, 2 vols., Lipsiae, 1885-1888.

Liber Sextus Decretalium D. Bonifacii Papae VIII, suae integritate una cum Clementinis et Extravagantibus, earumque Glossis restitutis, Romae, 1582.

Mansi, Joannes D., *Sacrorum Conciliorum Nova et Amplissima Collectio*, 53 vols. in 60, Parisiis, 1901-1927.

Potthast, Augustus, *Regesta Pontificum Romanorum inde ab anno post Christum natum MCXCVIII ad annum MCCCIV*, 2 vols., Berolini, 1874-1875.

Schroeder, H. J., *Canons and Decrees of the Council of Trent*, 3 ed., St. Louis: B. Herder, 1955.

REFERENCE WORKS

Abbo, John A.–Hannon, Jerome D., *The Sacred Canons*, revised ed., 2 vols., St. Louis: B. Herder, 1957.

Augustine, Charles, *A Commentary on the New Code of Canon Law*, 8 vols., Vol. VIII, 2. ed., *Penal Code*, St. Louis: B. Herder, 1924.

Ayrinhac, H. A.–Lydon, P. J., *Penal Legislation in the New Code of Canon Law*, revised ed., New York: Benziger, 1936.

Baart, Peter A., *Legal Formulary*, New York, 1898.

Bargilliat, Michael, *Praelectiones Iuris Canonici*, 37. ed., 2 vols., Parisiis, 1924.

Bartocetti, Victorius, *De Regulis Iuris Canonici*, Romae: Angelo Belardetti, 1955.

Bender, Ludovicus, *Normae Generales De Personis*, Romae: Desclée, 1957.

Berutti, Christopher, *Institutiones Iuris Canonici*, 6 vols., Vol. VI, *De Delictis et Poenis*, Taurini: Marietti, 1938.

Beste, Udalricus, *Introductio In Codicem*, 4. ed., Neapoli: D'Auria Pontificius, 1956.

Blat, Albertus, *Commentarium Textus Codicis Iuris Canonici*, 5 vols., Vol. 5, *De Delictis et Poenis*, Romae, 1924.

Bouscaren, T. L.–Ellis, A. C., *Canon Law, A Text and Commentary*, Milwaukee: Bruce, 1946.

Bouuaert, C.–Simenon, G., *Manuale Iuris Canonici*, 3 vols., Gandae et Leodii, 1943.

Capello, Felix, *Tractatus Canonico-Moralis De Censuris Iuxta Codicem Iuris Canonici*, 4. ed. emendata et aucta, Taurini: Marietti, 1950.

Casey, James V., *A Study of Canon 2222, § 1*, The Catholic University of America Canon Law Studies, n. 290, Washington, D. C.: The Catholic University of America Press, 1949.

Chelodi, J.–Ciprotti, P., *Ius Canonicum De Delictis et Poenis*, 5. ed. recognita et aucta, Trento: A. Ardesi, 1943.

Christ, Joseph J., *Dispensation From Vindictive Penalties*, The Catholic University of America Canon Law Studies, n. 174, Washington, D. C.: The Catholic University of America Press, 1943.

Cicognani, Amleto, *Canon Law*, 2. ed. revised, Westminister, Md.: Newman, 1934.

Clancy, Patrick, *The Local Religious Superior*, The Catholic University of America Canon Law Studies, n. 175, Washington, D. C.: The Catholic University of America Press, 1943.

Cloran, Owen, *Previews and Practical Cases, Delicts and Penalties*, Milwaukee: Bruce, 1951.

Cocchi, Guidus, *Commentarium in Codicem Iuris Canonici ad Usum Scholarum*, 8 vols., Vol. VIII, 4. ed., Taurinorum Augustae: Marietti, 1938.

Connor, Maurice, *The Administrative Removal of Pastors*, The Catholic University of America Canon Law Studies, n. 104, Washington, D. C.: The Catholic University of America, 1937.

Conran, Edward J., *The Interdict*, The Catholic University of America Canon Law Studies, n. 56, Washington, D. C.: The Catholic University of America, 1930.

Conte a Coronata, Mattheus, *Institutiones Iuris Canonici*, 4. ed., aucta et emendata, 5 vols., Taurini: Marietti, 1955.

Creusen, Joseph–Ellis, Adam, *Religious Men and Women in the Code*, 5. ed., Milwaukee: Bruce, 1953.

De Meester, Alphonsus, *Iuris Canonici et Iuris Canonico-Civilis Compendium*, nova editio, 3 vols. in 4, Brugis: Desclée, 1921-1928.

Droste, Francis,–Messmer, Sebastian, *Canonical Procedure in Disciplinary and Criminal Cases of Clerics*, New York, 1887.

Esswein, Anthony A., *The Extrajudicial Coercive Powers of Ecclesiastical Superiors*, The Catholic University of America Canon Law Studies, n. 127, Washington, D. C.: The Catholic University of America Press, 1941.

Fanfani, Ludovicus, *De Iure Religiosorum*, ed. altera revisa atque notabiliter aucta, Taurini: Marietti, 1925.

Ferreres, John, *Institutiones Canonicae*, 2 vols., Barcelona, 1920.

Findlay, Stephen, *Canonical Norms Governing the Deposition and Degradation of Clerics*, The Catholic University of America Canon Law Studies, n. 130, Washington, D. C.: The Catholic University of America Press, 1941.

Gasparri, Pietro, *Schema Codicis Iuris Canonici cum notis*, Romae, 1914.

Hostiensis (Henricus de Segusio), *Commentaria in Quinque Decretalium Libros*, 5 vols. in 3, Venetiis, 1581.

———, *Summa Aurea*, Lugduni, 1568.

Jone, Heribertus, *Commentarium in Codicem Iuris Canonici*, 3 vols., Paderborn: Officina Libraria F. Schöningh, 1950-1955.

Lega, Michael, *Praelectiones in Textum Iuris Canonici De Iudiciis Ecclesiasticis*, 4 vols., Vol. IV *De Iudiciis Criminalibus in Genere et in Specie, De Delictis et Poenis Praemisso Tractatu*, Romae: Typis Vaticanis, 1901.

Lega, M.–Bartoccetti, V., *Commentarius in Iudicia Ecclesiastica*, 3 vols., Romae: Anonima Libraria Cattolica Italiana, 1950.

Michiels, Gommarus, *De Delictis et Poenis*, Lublin-Polonia; Universitas Catholica, 1934.

———, *Principia Generalia De Personis In Ecclesia*, ed. altera, Romae: Desclée, 1955.

Migne, Jacques P., *Patrologiae Cursus Completus, Series Graeca*, 162 vols., Parisiis, 1856-1866.

———, *Patrologiae Cursus Completus, Series Latina*, 221 vols., Parisiis, 1844-1855.

O'Brien, Joseph, *The Exemption of Religious in Church Law*, Milwaukee: Bruce, 1943.

O'Brien, Raymond, *The Absolution of Recidivists in the Sacrament of Penance*, The Catholic University of America Studies in Sacred Theology, n. 76, Washington, D. C.: The Catholic University of America Press, 1943.

O'Brien, Romaeus W., *The Provincial Religious Superior*, The Catholic University of America Canon Law Studies, n. 258, Washington, D. C.: The Catholic University of America Press, 1947.

Ottaviani, Alaphridus, *Institutiones Iuris Publici Ecclesiastici*, 3. ed., 2 vols., Romae: Typis Polyglottis Vaticanis, 1947.

Panormitanus, Abbas (Nicholaus de Tudeschis), *Commentaria in Quinque Libros Decretalium*, 5 vols. in 7, Venetiis, 1588.

Prierias Sylvester (Mazolinus Sabaudus), *Summa Summarum*, Venetiis, 1601.

Prümmer, Dominicus, *Manuale Iuris Canonici*, 5. ed., Friburgi, 1927.

Quinn, Hugh G., *The Particular Penal Precept*, the Catholic University of America Canon Law Studies, n. 303, Washington, D. C.: The Catholic University of America Press, 1953.

Rainer, Eligius G., *Suspension of Clerics*, The Catholic University of America Canon Law Studies, n. 111, Washington, D. C.: The Catholic University of America, 1937.

Raus, J. B., *Institutiones Canonicae*, Parisiis, 1923.

Regatillo, Eduardus F., *Institutiones Iuris Canonici*, 4. ed., 2 vols., Sal Terrae: Santander, 1951.

Reiffenstuel, Anacletus, *Ius Canonicum Universum*, 7 vols., Parisiis, 1864-1870.

Ried—Brig, A., *Manuale Practicum Iuris Disciplinaris et Criminalis Regularium ad usum Ff. Minorum Capuccinorum*, Romae, 1902.

Roelker, Edward, *Precepts*, Paterson: St. Anthony Guild Press, 1955.

Romani, Sylvius, *Summa Iuris Canonici Lineamenta*, Romae, 1939.

Rufinus, *Summa Decretorum*, ed. Heinrich Singer, Paderborn, 1902.

Schaefer, Timotheus, *De Religiosis Ad Norman Codicis Iuris Canonici*, 4. ed., Romae: Apostolato Cattolico, 1947.

Schmalzgreuber, Franciscus, *Ius Ecclesiasticum Universum*, 5 vols. in 12, Romae, 1843-1845.

Schroeder, H. J., *Disciplinary Decrees of the General Councils*, St. Louis: B. Herder, 1937.

Sipos, Stephan, *Enchiridion Iuris Canonici*, Romae: B. Herder, 1954.

Smith, S. B., *Elements of Ecclesiastical Law*, 3. ed., 3 vols., Vol. III, *Ecclesiastical Punishments*, New York, 1888.

——— *New Procedure in Criminal and Disciplinary Causes of Ecclesiastics in the United States*, 2 .ed., New York, 1888.

Suarez, Franciscus, *Disputationum De Censuris in Communi*, Lugduni: Sumptibus Horatti Cardon, 1608.

Vermeersch, A.–Creusen, J., *Epitome Iuris Canonici,* 3 vols., Vol. III, 6 ed., Romae: H. Dessain, 1946.

Wernz, Franciscus X., *Ius Decretalium,* 3. ed., 6 vols., Vol. VI, *Ius Poenale Ecclesiasticae Catholicae,* Prati, 1913.

Wernz, F. X.–Vidal, P., *Ius Canonicum ad Codicis Normam Exactum,* 7 vols. in 8, Vol. III, *De Religiosis,* Romae: Societa Tipografica A. Macioce & Pisani, 1933; Vol. VII, *Ius Poenale Ecclesiasticum,* 2. ed., Romae: Typis Pontificiae Universitatis Gregorianae, 1951.

Woywod, Stanislaus, *A Practical Commentary on the Code of Canon Law,* 4. ed. revised, 2 vols., New York, 1932.

ALPHABETICAL INDEX

BIOGRAPHICAL NOTE

Paul Leo Love was born in Baltimore, Maryland on August 3, 1921. After receiving his primary education at Saint Thomas Aquinas parochial school and Mount Washington Country School, he attended Calvert Hall College for his high school course. Following this he enrolled at Loyola College, Baltimore and received the degree of Bachelor of Arts in 1943. In September of the same year he began studies for the priesthood, pursuing both the courses of philosophy and theology at Saint Mary's Seminary, Baltimore. He was ordained to the priesthood on June 12, 1947, and thereupon received a twofold appointment as Archivist of the Archdiocese of Baltimore and assistant pastor at All Saints parish. Shortly after ordination, he was assigned to a summer course of studies sponsored by American University in conjunction with the National Archives, Washington, D. C., and received a certificate in the Administration and Preservation of Archives. For the next nine years he served as Archivist and fulfilled the priestly duties of the parish ministry. In 1956 His Excellency Francis P. Keough, D. D., Archbishop of Baltimore, assigned him to the course of studies in the School of Canon Law at the Catholic University of America. He received the degree of the Baccalaureate in Canon Law in June, 1957, and the degree of the Licentiate in Canon Law in June, 1958. Upon completion of his doctoral studies in 1959, he received a temporary appointment as assistant pastor at Saint Joan of Arc parish, Aberdeen, Maryland.

CANON LAW STUDIES *

402. Chyang, Rev. Peter B., M. A., J. C. L., Decennial faculties for ordinaries in quasi-dioceses.
403. Gossman, Rev. Francis J., A. B., S. T. L., J. C. L., Pope Urban II and canon law.
404. Love, Rev. Paul L., A. B., J. C. L., The penal remedies of the Code of Canon Law.
405. McLeaish, Rev. Donald C., A. B., S. T. L., J. C. L., The Laws of the State of Texas affecting church property.
406. Rodriguez, Rev. Manuel J., Ph. B., S. T. L., J. C. L., The laws of the State of New Mexico affecting church property.
407. Sampon, Rev. Robert G., Ph. B., S. T. L., J. C. L., A comparative study of the First Provincial Council of Milwaukee and the Code of Canon Law.
408. Schreiber, Rev. Paul F., A. B., J. C. L., Canonical precedence.
409. Welsh, Rev. Maurice L., M. A., J. C. L., The laws of the State of Nevada affecting church property.

* For a complete list of the available numbers of this series apply to the Catholic University of America Press, 620 Michigan Ave., N. E., Washington (17), D. C. for a general catalogue.

www.ingramcontent.com/pod-product-compliance
Lightning Source LLC
LaVergne TN
LVHW050234080826
844660LV00012B/529